I Have Ears

LEARNING TO HEAR FROM GOD

Shawn Stutz

TABLE OF CONTENTS

PREFACE

This is really more than a book to me.

This is the story of how I came to fully appreciate
Jesus' invitation of "Come follow me."

These are not new words,
but they are words that have brought new life to me.

This is my adventure, both epic and irrelevant.
It may not be your journey,
but it may remind you of your journey.

The events in this story really happened,
and they could really happen to you.

ACKNOWLEDGMENTS

Writing a book is not easy. Don't get me wrong, there is great joy and fulfillment in the process of recording, for others, the truths and insights gleaned in a lifetime. However, it can also be a daunting task. With that said, I would be remiss not to mention those brothers and sisters in Christ that have encouraged me and blessed me along the way.

Before I share about people, I would like to first thank my great God and Savior, Jesus Christ. He has not only seen me through the tragedies and triumphs of my life, but He has given me the ability to share of His great grace toward me in words and story. Without a doubt, the power of the gospel of redemption has not been without great effect on my life.

I would like to thank my beautiful wife for always standing beside me in this adventure. Michelle, your words of encouragement have breathed more belief and confidence in me than you will ever know.

In the same vein, I would like to thank my kiddos, Kaitlyn and Elijah, for celebrating with me all the little successes I experienced during the writing process. This is a book I hope you take to heart, simply because it's the one thing I want you to know more than anything else: God wants to speak to your heart because He loves you immensely.

Additionally, I would like to express a great deal of gratitude to those that have supported this campaign with not only finances but with great amounts of prayer. Your blessings will never be forgotten. I only hope these words serve as a great big *thank you* as you read them.

Scott Elliott thank you for creating the cover art for the book. I love the cover! Doug Daniel, many thanks for your help with the second edition cover. Without you both I would have been left to make my own cover in *paint*. Please do not laugh. That is exactly what would have happened.

As this is the second edition of the book, I would like to thank the reader. Many have read the initial book, with its flaws, and not noticed anything. To you I say God bless you. The rest of you, who found what I call grammar goofs and typing joys, thank you as well. Your keen eyes and tough honesty have made this a better book.

If I can, I'd like to state how much re-releasing the book has emboldened me about the book's message and content. The rereading and revisionary processes have made me realize all the more that this work is most definitely the message of my heart and will remain that for the rest of my life.

Finally, I would like to extend a special thank you to Jon Byron, Chuck Miller, Alan Fadling, Paul Jensen, Craig Babb, and all of my Journey Generations and Leadership Institute family. The fellowship of the saints experienced in those environments, as well as the depth of wisdom discovered, cannot be overstated as one of the greatest contributors to my own personal discipleship. A mere thank you is not enough.

I pray that you enjoy this book, and even more so I pray you enjoy the Lord who so changed my life and invited me to share this transformation story with others.

~ Shawn Stutz

INTRODUCTION
I Have Ears

He who has ears to hear, let him be listening and let him consider and perceive and comprehend by hearing. ~ Matthew 11:15 AMP

I often visit my local coffee-shop bookstore. I like to call it my "second office." There is a little nook in the back with enough chairs to provide the privacy needed for me to truly concentrate. It's in the Art/Interior Design/You-Name-It for Dummies section. There, among the pages of thousands of other authors is where many of these pages were birthed. Along with other bookstore junkies, the curiosity magazine hunter, and the occasional socially awkward shopper, I sit and allow the classical music overhead to feed my creativity. The dull roar of espresso machines, the stocking of shelves, and the murmur of conversations all fade away as I disappear into my own world of thought.

Thankfully I have learned to selectively tune out the mother correcting her children, the guy chatting up business on his cell phone, and even the clicking of my computer keys. It's amazing how much actual noise is going on around me and all I hear, or choose to hear, is my own inner voice (which sounds much more radio-friendly than my own).

Hearing truly is a powerful sense. Though I have nearly mastered the art of selective listening while at my "second office," I found myself distractingly captivated one day. Taking up most of the outdoor seating of the bookstore was a group of people who were gesturing strongly with their hands. I, being at a distance on the other side of a pane glass window began to imagine the worst. *There is about to be a fight*, was all I could think. My fear over the scene before me quickly shifted to personal embarrassment. Although I didn't make the connection at first, I soon realized the people outside the glass were deaf.

A World on Mute

Deafness and the Deaf Community intrigue me. I once stumbled on a website promoting an upcoming Deaf Community convention. *What would that be like for the hearing person?* I wondered. I imagined a convention hall of silence minus the shuffling of feet, a commercial air conditioning fan, and the rustling of program guide pages. I'm sure that's a bit hyper-stereotypical, but either way, this convention's website highlighted my extreme auditory dependence.

Growing up in Ohio, my family would often make the trek to my hometown of Buffalo, New York to visit my grandmothers. Of course, we did the normal kid stuff; we complained about the smell, groaned after eating sugar-free candy, and explored the attic full of ancient stuff. My cousin Keith would occasionally be there. Keith is deaf.

I remember the strange feeling of not knowing how to act around him, and the times I would be reminded he could not hear me talking. That's difficult for a kid. Eye contact and attentiveness in conversation are hard enough for an adult. Imagine a kid trying to master that art and not knowing what to do once eye contact was made. I did not know sign language. I felt helpless. *Why couldn't he hear?* I thought. *He has ears.*

> *"God gave us two ears and one mouth, so we can hear twice as much as we say."*
> *- Anonymous*

Just like moments with my cousin, the time spent watching the deaf community at my second office stuck out to me. I sat in my wooden chair imagining what it would be like to be outside with them, to be non-hearing. I wouldn't have heard the impatient car honks from the lunch hour traffic swooshing by quickly. I would not notice the concrete scratching noise caused by metal chairs being slid into their circle of conversation. That inviting voice and quip-ish conversation with the friendly barista would be reduced to basic pointing and courteous head nods. The courteous "pardon me" to pass by someone might go unnoticed or be mistakenly perceived as rudeness. The miscellaneous noise of music, cell phones, and kids crying would be non-existent. It would be a world on mute.

Deliberate, Get-to-the-Point Listening

My thoughts were whirling. I tried to figure out what this group was saying to each other. I somehow thought I could interpret the flurry of hand motions. However, the pace and similarity of the motions had me clueless. For whatever reason, I imagined their conversation was loftier than the basic pleasantries or random musings that my friends and I would have. I am not so sure why I felt that way. It is just that each word seemed so much more deliberate, more of a "get-to-the-point" kind of communication. True attentiveness to the vocabulary of motion appeared to be more demanding than just mumbling about work and the weather.

A few more minutes went by when it struck me, they too have ears. They have ears and can't hear, but there is so much listening still happening. It's not the same type of listening I am accustomed to, but it is listening nonetheless.

Listening is hearing plus understanding plus remembering.

It may be naivety, but it seems that losing the intricate ability to process sound into language would enhance one's true ability to listen. The deaf must stay tuned to the people they are conversing with. If not, life and relationships would soon be reduced to a series of waving hands and quiet space. The language of the listening deaf is one that is unique to their community alone. No other people group on the planet is dependent on reading lips and significant hand signals alone. This concept translates onto every continent too. Love may be the universal language; however, sign language cannot be too far behind.

In the summer of 2000, I spent ten days in Rio de Janeiro, Brazil listening to the beautiful language of Portuguese all around me. Even though I was only slightly versed in High School Spanish and Mexican restaurant menu, I was able to gain enough understanding of the sounds I heard, in context, to follow the flow of worship songs, taxi-cab bartering, and basic chit-chat. However, take me to a convention of the Deaf and I'd be clueless. I need noise, vocal patterns, and inflection to stand a chance at understanding. Even then I would struggle to listen well, and I have ears that work.

I wonder if today's church suffers from a similar problem? She has ears, but has the art of listening been lost? Don't get me wrong, she can hear. She can hear very well. She has heard the loud bellows of the traditionalists and the "sound theology" monitors. The endless diatribe of fabulous fads, wonder strategies, and life-changing programs regularly contribute to the noise. Rock-star pastors and lower-tier wannabe's jockey for their turn at the microphone in a way that would cause the apostle Paul to write a letter or two. One cannot forget the yelping of televangelists shouting promises of health and wealth in exchange for enough faith. I have a feeling Paul, in one of those new letters, would pen a few beating and shipwreck stories for today's contemporaries to ponder.

Plus the church can't escape the plethora of conferences designed for modern church innovators, all of which are clamoring for our attention. Church program strategists and para-church justice-based platforms join the conversation along with their social media entourage. Add in the minor chord of "music-style worship-wars" to the constant crescendo of the church soundtrack and it's easy to see why believers today struggle to hear the voice of God.

How can one hear the still, small voice of the Creator in the midst of a raging subculture sound barrage?

On top of that, we have the lies of the evil one; perpetually strong, delivered to us daily in uniquely enticing packages. It is no wonder so many miss the whisper of our Divine Lover. The crowd is just too loud. The carnival of Christianity has almost joined in the carnality of culture and slowly drowned out the voice of our Great God.

We, the church, have ears. We just have not learned to hear Him speak. All too often our hearts and souls are deaf. Unlike those born without the ability to hear, the church can be awakened. The voice of the Lord can speak to the soul deaf and bring miraculous new life, and that in itself is truly good news.

QUESTIONS FOR THE CHURCH TODAY

So what is one to do?
What should be the response of the church?
How does the bride hear the wooing of her lover
through the shouting of other suitors?

These are great questions. In fact, I would say these are the biggest questions for the church right now. Without a return to the much-needed practice of divine listening, congregations around the country will dry up at alarming rates.

Now to be fully clear about the drying of congregations, church attendance won't fully reflect this phenomenon. No, many a Christian is contented enough with the formula of religion and the entertaining production of weekend worship. Their numb hearts prickle awake following a rousing attack on immorality or an emotional musical number. But by Tuesday morning the dry thirst of the soul returns, a thirst that cannot be quenched by man. Many are compelled back to the building for a midweek dose of Messiah-like medicine. Others may tough it out until the weekend. Then it is smile at the door where greeted and make your way to the seat defeated.

The cycle is never-ending. If you don't believe me, ask the majority of your local congregation where they felt the Lord's presence this week—and don't count Bible studies and ministry events as an answer. Ask them, *"What was the last thing you know, for sure, the Lord spoke to you?"* Ask about their perceived feelings of intimacy with Christ—and don't allow the *quantity* of quiet times to satisfy that question. Then probe into people's Scripture reading moments. Will they articulate truths that deepen one's relationship with the divine or will the consensus be that they simply checked a box?

No, churches won't slack off too much in attendance, but people will dry up on the inside. They are hungry for intimacy with Christ yet are nearly starving in the consumer model of today's church. Believers will use the church as Advil to make the pains of the world subside. Pastors will keep offering events, challenge for will-powered commitments, and count filled seats instead of vibrantly discipled souls as success. All the while, God will keep speaking.

The Church, Christ's Bride,
She has ears, but is She listening?

The reason I'm compelled to write this story is because both the unintentional and the volitional soul deafness I have described are part of my spiritual journey. I would venture to say it is a part of your journey, too. You and I, along with every other human on the planet, whether any of us knows it or not, crave for the Creator to speak to our hearts. My hope is that these pages will serve as both an encouragement and a strong invitation to you. Throughout your reading adventure, you will hear my story, and I'm almost certain you will see your story in the midst.

Through learning to listen to the heavenly Father, my life has been revolutionized on three major levels: personally, communally, and vocationally. Each of these three components will be unpacked in the pages ahead, along with practical points of application that will invite active listeners into to greater levels of intimacy with Jesus.

Above all, I hope you begin to sense the voice of the Lord with greater and greater clarity. I truly hope you will be able to read between the lines of my story and see how God is wooing you into His greater story. Without a doubt, I can attest to the fact that learning to know and follow the voice of the Great Shepherd has been more than worth it. Let's get started, or in the words of Jesus, *"He who has ears, let him hear"* (Mark 4:9).

Part One

Personally

- 1 -
LEARNING TO LOVE GOD

You shall love the Lord your God with all your heart and
with all your soul and with all your might. ~ Deuteronomy 6:5 ESV

"Because God has made us for Himself, our hearts
are restless until they rest in Him." ~ Augustine of Hippo

I grew up at church. Well, actually I grew at home, but I remember going to church quite often. My parents came to a saving faith when I was in preschool. Marcie was the name of the woman that introduced my parents to a personal relationship with Jesus. Although my parents were raised with an understanding of the saving work of Jesus under the direction of the Catholic Church, much of their religious experiences were that of duty and fear.

Marcie worked with my mother at the local nursing home. Marcie also attended the Southern Baptist church across the street from my preschool. It was during these days, when I was more fixated on the Dukes of Hazard than faith, that my mother and father discovered the emptiness of a culturally religious lifestyle minus a life surrendered to the Savior.

As time went on, Sundays became very important in the Stutz house. It was truly a time to honor the Sabbath. We would put on our best church clothes, march into separate Sunday School classes and then transition to the worship service together. The building itself was the typical Baptist brick, stained glass windows, and leftover 1970s wood-panel decor. As one might imagine, the platform was clad with the traditional pulpit, choir loft, and baptismal pool (you are not inside a true Baptist church unless there is a baptismal front and center). To the left and right of the pulpit were the time-honored instruments of worship; the piano and the organ. The pews were lightly-padded wooden benches, complete with a hymnal and Bible rack mounted on the back. The Lord's house became our house every Sunday morning.

My family sat near the front of the sanctuary every week. After a musical call to worship from the piano and organ, or on special days, a prelude from the choir, we would be greeted, prayed over, and then shake hands with the people in the pews around us. Next came the songs of worship. We would sing from the hymnal while the music man would wave his hand at us. I remember, as a kid, being confused at his hand motions. I had never seen anyone else wave at people while they sang. Either way, I would watch his hand; ceiling, floor, window, door, and repeat.

There were songs that sounded more dirge-like with the heavy tone of the organ while others felt more like anthems of sincere faith. During those songs, the voices grew louder and a few people in the choir even smiled. It was not long before I was memorizing these musical standards and their page numbers in the hymnal. It became a game of memory for me trying to guess the song or hymn number before the music minister would announce it aloud.

If theology is the study of God, then I was studying God at an early age via The Baptist Hymnal. I learned that I was a wretch and only at the old rugged cross was that changed. I discovered that Baptists, and I guess God, liked blood a lot more than I did. Let's just say that I was not that keen on the image of being washed in the blood of the lamb as a kid— nor today for that matter.

Something even more foundational was happening during our times of praise and worship. I was learning theology.

I also learned the concept of a lofty, holy, and powerful being who was greater than anything or anyone in the known universe. Most important, I learned how this grand God wanted to walk with me and talk with me and tell me I was His own. Hymns were a huge part of my pre-conversion development.

After the sing-along portion of the service was over, the choir would sing its "special music" for the week while we got a chance to place money in the plate. I had the special privilege of placing the offering envelope in the metal plate as it came by. For the record, the deacons who collected the offering always made me feel nervous. It seemed that only after your giving was deposited would you get their quiet nod of approval.

Pastor Glenn and the Pointy Finger

Pastor Glenn Hicks was the pastor of our Baptist church and he would deliver a word from the Lord each week. Pastor Glenn was a tough-looking man, at least to a six-year-old. He was a great man of God, plus he had a firm handshake to go with it. His straightforward, deliberate demeanor matched his physical appearance. In the purest form of the word, Pastor Glenn was a preacher and preach he did. With one hand he would hold the edge of the pulpit. With the other, he would reach around the pulpit and point to us while driving home his points.

I do not remember the content of many of Glenn's messages, but what I do remember was his passion. Pastor Glenn was passionate about God, about people going to heaven, and pointing his finger. It was this passion with which he punctuated his sermons that not only caught my attention but my parent's as well.

My dad would occasionally grunt in affirmation while my mom would voice "Amen." They would both follow along in the Bible as he read, underlining or highlighting key words or phrases as he spoke. Dad would lean forward and listen; one knee propping up his arm, the other holding up his Bible. He seemed so fixated during the teaching time that it made me all the more curious. If Pastor Hick's words were that important to my father, it had to be a big deal.

Of course, I learned about the life and ministry of Jesus in the gospels. Christmas brought cantatas and the telling of the reason for the season; unto us a child was born. As a young kid, I loved hearing about the miracles Jesus performed, especially the feeding of the five thousand. During my teen years, I loved that Jesus bucked the system, challenged the status quo even. I was always impressed when he would flip the vindictive questions of the Pharisees right back on them. The finale of the Good Friday cross and Easter's empty tomb wrapped up the church calendar so the life of Jesus was always fresh in my mind.

The New Testament introduced me to Paul's great missionary journeys. From shipwrecks to miracles, prison escapes to stand-offs with government leaders, Paul was the wild renegade of the early church era. I also found it very intriguing that he could perform some of the same miracles as Jesus; same Spirit, same power. His writings were good, despite his love for prepositional phrases. I must admit that he did seem to fuss a lot at church people. Churches back then must have been a real mess (please catch my tongue-in-cheek tone).

On the flip side, the Old Testament introduced me to the Israelites and the great stories of the faith. I learned about characters like Moses, Abraham, King David, and the men of the fiery furnace.

However, one of the biggest things I remember was that anyone without a relationship with Jesus Christ would spend eternity without Him in hell. Hell was, well hell. It was the place of endless torment, where people would forever wail and gnash their teeth. It was the only place without God's love, forgiveness, peace, and kindness in His entire created universe.

God did not technically send people to hell. No, people chose to go there and spend an eternity suffering with the devil and his angels. Why? I did not know, but that is what I heard people did. To put it bluntly, messages about an afterlife without God's love scared the hell out of me. I remember deciding that I was not going to hell, ever, no matter what it took.

Salvation Is Here

I recall my salvation experience took place on my bed. It was a small bed, clad in Star Wars sheets. I suppose it was a foreshadowing of the spiritual warfare I would experience from the dark side later in life (you can smile at that if you want— it's really not that sacrilegious).

After asking a series of questions to my parents at home, they came to the conclusion that I was ready to begin a relationship with Jesus. Mom and dad asked Pastor Glenn to come over to confirm their belief and lead me in a prayer of salvation. He did. I prayed right there on my Star Wars sheets and Luke Skywalker held up his light saber in defiance to the kingdom of darkness while I did.

All kidding aside, I knew the sincerity of my heart had united me with God and rescued me from hell. Little did I know what whole new world had just opened up to me. I was about to spend the rest of my life on the planet getting to know and love the lofty, holy God who washed me in blood and wanted to walk with me.

I grew up in a denomination where the Scriptures were highly elevated. If you didn't know better you would have thought the Bible had somehow joined the Holy Trinity. Don't get me wrong, I love the Word of God immensely. It is just that more often than not I heard "the Bible says" instead of "our God says."

This, of course, enforced the subtle mistruth that we should listen more to what a Bible teacher says rather than God himself. Though not the intention, it simply reinforced that I was not truly able to read the Bible and hear God's voice on my own. To really understand the Scriptures, I needed a pastor, a Sunday School teacher or a printed workbook to guide me through the text.

There were times when I felt like God seemed to speak to me individually. It was Him challenging me with wisdom in Proverbs. It was Him confronting my sin, like the sin of Israel, in the stories of the Kings and the Judges. He Himself moved me to live holy through the writings of Paul. He both scared and comforted me a little at the reading of Revelation. Through the words penned by Holy Spirit inspired men, I fell in love with God. Yet, at some point, my desire for God was traded away for a simpler, less personal transfer of information.

My knowledge of the word grew even more through church events like camps and the ever popular Vacation Bible School. Every time a teacher would ask a question about the Scriptures, it was like a game of trivial pursuit to me. I wanted to be the first to shout out the answer. I participated in Bible Drill challenges as well. In these drills, we turned the Bible into a competition. Who could find a specific verse first? Who could name the five books of the Pentateuch? Who could name the New Testament books in order?

My time in the Scriptures began to lean toward knowledge of about God, not the Living God Himself.

Though Bible Drill was all about memorizing truths from God's Word, very little "hiding them in our hearts that we might not sin against the Lord" (Psalm 119:11) was happening. My time in the scriptures definitely leaned toward the knowledge about God and not a relationship with God Himself.

23

I soon discovered people praise good boys in church. With the knowledge I had stored up about the Bible, along with my involvement in everything, I was well on my way to being a good church boy. In the church, good boys grow up to be good men. How many times have you heard one congregant describe a man in church as "Well, he's a really good guy." As silly as that seems to sound, that was my goal. Therefore, my pursuit of goodness and moral behavior took precedence.

However, I do not recall Jesus telling the little children around him, or the disciples for that matter, to be good boys and girls. No, He said, "Love the Lord with all your heart, soul, mind and body." That is a statement of being first, behavior second. Being is not the fruit of a tree, but its root. Being alters the externals of life, but only by yielding to a divine transformation of the internals.

Don't get me wrong, good moral behavior is not bad. It's just that when the deacons were chosen to serve the widows in the early church, Luke writes that they were men full of the Holy Spirit (Acts 6:5). When the Pharisees spoke of the disciples in the book of Acts, they didn't use the words "good man" to describe them. No, they were stunned by their authority and power, as men who had been with Jesus. They weren't simply "good men." Instead, they were wretched men, transformed by the goodness of God because of their internal belief and faith in Jesus and His coming Kingdom— a kingdom with a scandalous message of grace and redemption.

When you think of your life as an ambassador for the King of the Universe, who wants to settle for just being "good"? Well, unfortunately, I did. I learned my Bible facts. I attended every possible church activity. I even volunteered to serve at church in the ways that I could. I was a good boy and people saw that. But the eyes that saw my external goodness would become a bit sharper when my father surrendered to the ministry.

My dad became a pastor when I was in junior high. Junior high is such an awkward transitional life stage anyway. So, when your dad becomes the pastor of small town church in central Missouri, things get really awkward. I did not realize the change his vocational calling would bring on our family, or me individually. People joke about pastor's kids, but it is not always the easiest gig.

Of course, my dad took a smaller income, seemed to work more, carried the burdens of more people, and led a church struggling to know its real purpose. As a family, we would all soon realize that was pretty normal when it came to ministry. What I did not expect was my sudden fixation with having to perfect. Perfection was the unwritten rule for pastor's kids, or so I thought.

Looking back on the whole season of wrestling with goodness over godliness, I wish I had had the wisdom to realize my role as a representative of God to my friends. My calling was no different than that of my father. His positional leadership didn't supersede my relationship leadership. Just because he was a pastor did not make him more holy or greater than I could potentially be. It did, of course, make him more aware of his calling every day (we will address more of this idea later). Either way, without a proper understanding of calling, the next phase of my life proved to be a confusing and often difficult one.

The fish bowl life now created for me led to an even deeper devotion to religious performance.

If my external behaviors of "good man-ness" had to be front and center before, then being a pastor's kid meant they were definitely on display. Even while I struggled with sin internally or acted out sinful behaviors in secret, there was a droning voice in the back of my mind saying, "the show must go on."

I later learned that I wasn't the only one who felt this way about religion and life. You may even have felt, or still do feel that undue pressure. As a fledgling teenager, I found the pressure taxing, or better yet exhausting. Whether truly expected of me or not, I sought to be perfect in the eyes of everyone. If there was a positive to this lifestyle, my external morality was above average. Religiously, I checked all the church boxes, figuratively and literally. Sunday School forms scored my church attendance, offering, Bible in hand, and bonus points for occasionally bringing a friend.

However, inside I was a wreck. I knew the struggles of sin and selfishness that plagued my heart and mind. I knew my restless doubts about God that sent me spinning. And if pleasing people was not hard enough, pleasing God was near impossible. I can vividly remember concentrating so hard on not sinning so Jesus would not be disappointed with me. Just like Adam and Eve in the garden hiding in fig leaves, I was endlessly trying to hide the shame of my sin. I had not fully realized that Jesus, in his infinite grace, had embraced my shame on the cross and discarded it at the tomb so I could be forever free.

Instead, somewhere deep inside I had developed a thought that God would be upset with me for putting him on the cross. This was the worst inception of thought for one who truly desired a relationship with the living God. I wanted to keep his commands, it is just that I could not do it perfect enough or with a high enough frequency for my liking.

The Silver Lining and the Dark Cloud

Despite the internal struggle with sin and shame and the external pageantry that took place, my knowledge and love of God grew in this season. That may seem strange after everything else you have just read, but it is true.

I remember reading the Scriptures and being amazed. I recall praying often for people, future moments, church member illness, and my deep desire to please God. Musical artists provided a steady diet of spiritual inspiration. Camps and conferences would stoke the fire of devotion once again and lead me to approach the throne of God with confidence for a season. Soul growth was most assuredly taking place. This growth, little as it was, became the silver lining in the midst of my darkness and brokenness.

It was not that I did not want to love God more, it was just that I did not fully understand His immense love for me yet.

However, the one thing that I was missing was an appreciation of hearing His voice. Although I studied God's commands, I did not really know His voice. The Good Shepherd was most assuredly calling, but I was not attuned to His speaking. I had embarked on a journey of spiritual revelation without real relationship. I had taken the Experiencing God courses, but I had not truly experienced Him in an abiding way like Moses and his colleague Joshua.

I would venture to say that many in the Christian community today suffer from a similar syndrome. They talk to God. They know of God and His commands. They even have moving moments with

God. But as a whole, they would say they do not hear from Him, or they cannot articulate what He has spoken to them. This may even be true of you.

What made this condition worse for me were the great stories of the Bible. The more I read them the more I found myself jealous of great Bible figures that had amazing conversations with God. Nothing messes with your quest for perfection quite like being jealous of how dead and gone saints of the faith interacted intimately with God. As you can see I was a mess, but at least to God, it was a beautiful mess.

QUESTIONS TO PONDER

What is your spiritual heritage? How was faith a part of your upbringing, if at all?

How did you come to a saving faith in Jesus Christ? What is your testimony?

How did your church worship experiences shape you? How did they hinder or help your development as a believer?

Did you ever wrestle with living in a Christian fish bowl?

Did you ever or do you currently struggle to have a sincere relationship with God, to hear His voice speaking to your heart?

Do you ever feel like you are a spiritual mess? Do you, at the same time, believe Jesus sees that spiritual mess as beautiful vulnerability?

- 2 -
HE-MAN AND BIBLE HEROES

Thus the Lord used to speak to Moses face to face,
as a man speaks to his friend. When Moses turned again
into the camp, his assistant Joshua the son of Nun, a young man,
would not depart from the tent. ~ Exodus 33:11 ESV

"Give me 100 preachers who fear nothing but sin and desire nothing
but God; such alone will shake the gates of hell." ~ John Wesley

When I was a boy, I played with He-Man toys. For those of you who have only known the internet and high-tech gaming systems, He-Man was the self-proclaimed Master of the Universe. Not only was he the action figure of my era, right behind G.I. Joe, he was the animated hero of my Saturday mornings as well.

Without fail, during each episode, He-Man would raise his big sword and yell out his name, striking fear in the hearts of his enemies. After which he would ride his green tiger, Battle-Cat, to fend off the villainous attacks of Skeletor and his evil gang. Thinking of this right now makes me realize how impressionable I was then, but nevertheless, He-Man was my Saturday morning cartoon hero (followed closely by the G.I. Joe, of course).

As my parents grew in their faith, the more they felt the wild witchcraft of He-Man and his entourage needed to go. Thankfully, G.I. Joe made the cut. As much as I did not fully understand the reasoning then, I am thankful that my heroes became more than a sword-wielding muscle-man. Instead of He-Man, there was Samson. Instead of the evil Skeletor, there were the Philistines. The bonus was every one of my new heroes had a relationship with the true Master of the Universe. They spoke with God. They responded to God. One of the men, Jacob, even wrestled with God.

While I was younger I remember being amazed and enthralled at these biblical heroes. Yet as an adult, and occasionally still today, I find myself jealous of the men and women of the Bible; those that talked with God so directly. Not only did they speak to Him, but they received profound messages from God that led to great faith, great adventures, and great intimacy with God Himself. Walk with me through a few of these stories to see what I mean.

Abraham

Take for instance the Genesis account of father Abraham, or Abram for short. Abram lived in Ur of the Chaldeans and had a fairly successful life. He was married to Sarai. His extended family lived nearby. Business was going well. But there was a distinct difference between Abram and his neighbors. Abram and Sarai had no children. Plus, they were aged well beyond the years of being with child.

One can empathize with Sarai and Abram to an extent. The sadness of not being able to have children would cut deep. These feelings would be even more amplified in the Hebrew context. In Abram's day, before a better understanding of eternity provided by Jesus' death and resurrection was available, the concept of everlasting life was tied very much to one's descendants. The taller and wider your family tree went, the more your name would never be forgotten. The more children a family had, the more they would, in a sense, live on from generation to generation. However, our forefather in the faith could not become a father to flesh.

Yet in the midst of Abram's childless days, Yahweh brings him a message. Yahweh is the English transliteration of the Hebrew name for God which literally means "I Am;" denoting the ever-present eternality of God. Yahweh's message to Abram came in the form of a covenant. It involved renaming Abram, which means "father," to Abraham, which when translated is "father of many nations."

God proceeds to share with Abraham about how he will one day have descendants that outnumber the sands on the shore and the stars in the sky. That is a lot of descendants where I come from. That had to be both great and challenging news for a childless man. Although it took quite a few years for even the initiation of that promise to occur, God kept His promise to Abraham and made him the father of the nations of Israel. Wouldn't you love to have the Lord promise something that amazing about your life? I don't know about you, but I would take even half as amazing a promise.

At yet another time, God sent messengers to Abraham to tell him of the coming destruction of the cities of Sodom and Gomorrah. Unfortunately, Sodom is where Lot, Abraham's nephew, lived. In a series of intercessory interactions, Abraham pleaded with God to withhold the destruction coming on the wicked cities. However, the needed righteousness of Sodom and Gomorrah was not found and the twin cities were reduced to ashes in the form of fiery judgment from heaven. Despite the unintended outcome, it is powerful to consider that Abraham got an opportunity to talk with, at best, the pre-incarnate Christ, and at least, an angel of God. That would be something I would sign up for given the chance.

Noah

Consider Noah. He received a message from the Lord to build a boat in order to save his family from the coming destruction of a flood on all the nations of the earth. *A boat, in the middle of the desert?* Yes, a boat. Can you imagine the potential for Noah to possibly doubt God? Yet with great confidence, Noah built the ark and gathered the animals into it in order to keep them and his family safe from the flood.

Would you like God to contact you in this way? Some would say yes, but the better question is would you like God to invite you to do something as crazy as building Noah's floating houseboat and zoo? Something makes me think that we just might be too comfortable with the status quo of our lives to really treasure that kind of interruption. Nevertheless, I find myself somewhat jealous of Noah's adventures on the high seas, or at least the invitation to it.

Moses

Look at the life of Moses. He spoke to God more intimately than probably anyone in the Bible outside of Jesus Himself. He heard the Redeemer in a bush of fire. He spoke to God atop Mount Sinai. Plus, the Scriptures also teach that he saw the glory of God's backside while hidden in the cleft of a rock. Moses received the Ten Commandments. He interceded on behalf of the people of Israel, saving countless lives. For forty days he spent time with Yahweh conversing about the Law of God. Moses even conversed with God in the highly regarded Tent of Meeting (Exodus 33). There, according to the text, Moses spoke with God face to face as a man would speak with his friend.

Do you desire divine engagements like that of Moses for your life?
Do you feel even the slightest twinge of jealousy toward Moses?
How would you like a burning bush experience?
Would you be up for a forty-day conversation initiated by God?

Joshua

Joshua was the leader of God's people in the Exodus alongside Moses. He, too, spoke with God face to face in the Tent of Meeting. After Moses died, it was Joshua that was charged with guiding the nation of Israel to the promise land. Do not forget how the angel of the Lord met with Joshua the evening before the battle of Jericho to give him a wild and wacky plan by which to seize the walled city. Joshua's listening and obedience led to a rousing victory over Israel's enemies at Jericho (Joshua 6).

How would you like to receive clear plans, crazy or otherwise, for the next major obstacle in your life? Better yet, how great would it be if they were delivered to you by an angel? I believe my obedience level would rise to the occasion if angels delivered messages to me on a more regular basis. I don't know about you, but I get a little jealous of just about anyone in the Bible that got to chat with angels about the future work of God in his or her life. I would love an angel to draw my attention to my need for divine dependence during my next life trial.

Paul

I even find myself jealous of Saul, the persecutor of the church, when Jesus confronts him on the way to Damascus. Yes, I know that God knocks him off a horse, blinds him for a few days, and changes his name to Paul that he might become a missionary to Jews and Gentiles alike. However, an unbelievable encounter with God like that rivals even the most intimate exchange I have ever had with Jesus.

32

Peter, James, and John

What about the disciples? How can you not help but be jealous of them, especially Peter, James, and John? These three men saw the transfiguration, the resurrection of multiple dead people, the changing of water to wine, and the calming of the seas. They heard explanations of the parables, received descriptive teachings on the kingdom of God, and so on and so on. These men saw it all, smelled it all, and heard it all. They traveled with Jesus throughout the course of His entire earthly ministry.

Can you imagine the wonder of sitting with Jesus as He taught? Now I love specific teachers, and I would say that God uses their abilities to expound His word to be a blessing in my life. However, there have been none anywhere near equal to Jesus, the Son of God, breaking down my misunderstandings of the kingdom.

The List Goes On and On...

There are countless other biblical characters that have stirred, and continue to stir up, a bit of jealousy in me. No, it is not an evil jealousy. Instead, it is a desire that I would be the one spoken to or the hope that I could hear divine directives from God. Take Jonah for example. Jonah, a prophet of God, although stubborn and completely ungrateful, still heard from God; in his house, in a fish, in a city, and on a hill. If you add in a box with a fox, Jonah would be the Dr. Suess of hearing from God despite his bad attitude and reluctant missionary willingness.

There is no voice like the voice of He who calms the waves to speak comfort and conviction to my heart.

Elijah stood before a holy barbecue pit, prayed to God, and Jehovah answered with fire from the sky. How is that for a reply to your prayers? Nothing seems to turn the question mark of faith into an exclamation point of solid belief like a raging inferno from the heavens.

Jacob, later named Israel, wrestled with God and refused to tap out. He received a life-long limp, but he also received a blessing from God. He spoke to Yahweh and Yahweh spoke back in a profoundly amazing way. Can you imagine the spiritual conversation starter Jacob had when it came to witnessing? Someone might say to him, "Ouch Jacob, it looks like that fight messed you up." To which Jacob could easily reply, "Yes, but you should see the other guy. No seriously, you should really meet God." Priceless!

How could you not be a little jealous of these biblical figures? They experienced a real closeness with God. Let me be very honest. That jealousy, whether innocent or not, is wrong. Jealousy like that stems from believing the lie that God does not want to deliver a fresh word of truth to us today. Sadly, this lie has sabotaged my divine listening all too often during my Christian journey.

However, I remember one day in particular when everything I thought I knew about listening to God suddenly changed. God came closer than He ever had and my jealousy of Bible characters almost all but fluttered away.

QUESTIONS TO PONDER

Can you relate? Have you ever found yourself feeling a little jealous of Bible characters and their exciting encounters with God?

How do you desire to hear God most? Would you like an angel or a message from a pastor or a prophet? Do you hope to hear God speak to you through the power of a mighty miracle?

Are you okay with God whispering His will for you in a still, small voice?

What is a time when you know you distinctly heard God speak to you in a profound way? How could you be certain it was truly God?

- 3 -
IT'S NOT DAGOBAH,
BUT I MAY HAVE FOUND YODA

In the same way, you who are younger,
submit yourselves to your elders. ~ 1 Peter 5:5a NIV

"The one indispensable requirement for producing godly, mature
Christians is godly, mature Christians." ~ Kevin DeYoung

In second grade I wanted to be Luke Skywalker. Then again I grew up in an era when just about every young boy introduced to the Star Wars saga wanted to be Luke Skywalker. My school recess times were filled with far off galaxy reenactments, along with a few made-up adventures as well. I was always Luke, because of the blonde hair. My buddy with brown hair was cast as Han Solo, and the one tomboy girl of the class, who would agree to play with us, filled the role of Leia. Occasionally our friends Boba Fett and Chewbacca would join in.

Without fail, during our half hour of leisure, we always fought off the dark side and its evil empire. Inevitably, Darth Vader would fatefully come to try and ruin our plans, and the ever-wise Yoda would then praise us for a job well done. The celebration of our victories took place over the wonder of cafeteria pizza and canned corn on a tray. I love those memories.

Maybe it was the Star Wars indoctrination or something a little more profound, but I have always longed for a Yoda in my life. I always looked for someone who would take me under their wing and teach me how to live and be successful. Of course, my parents did that

I've always looked for someone who would take me under their wing and teach me how to live and be successful.

to a certain degree. However, I believe there is something deep inside of us all that wants that "other-than-parent" person to fill the Yoda-mentor role as well. I wanted to be believed in by someone outside my family. I desired to be apprenticed, challenged, and nurtured. A small number of people had come close to filling that longing in my life. However, it was not until a ministry adventure took my family and me westward to Modesto, California that this long-seeded desire became a reality.

In 2006, I accepted a position as the Pastor to College and Young Adults at Big Valley Grace Community Church (yes, my business card was wide). My wife and I packed up the house and kiddos and relocated from the mountains of beautiful Northern Georgia to the dry Central Valley desert of Northern California. Let's just say that this was not only a geographic shock but a culture shock as well. My wife had never lived out of the South before and we were more than twelve hours from the closest member of our family. No one said "y'all" and we were nowhere near a Chick-fil-a or Cracker Barrel. What were we to do?

To assist with our journey, the church hired a moving company to relocate our stuff, which took up one-fourth of a semi-trailer. I remember laughing at that the sight of it, but the simplistic side of me was glad. After the trailer was loaded, my wife and young kids went to visit family in Knoxville, Tennessee. The plan was that they would later fly out to begin our new west coast life.

I, on the other hand, was left to drive our car the near 3000 miles to Modesto by myself. My Georgia license was set to expire in three days and I was not about to renew in one state only to have to purchase a new one in California. Needless to say, the clock was on. I had three days to complete the daunting cross-country trek. To make matters worse, day one of the journey was my thirtieth birthday.

Now I know that most people cringe, groan, or fear their forties. As I am now approaching that day, I can see why. However, I was in a massive state of depression the day I turned thirty. The main reason was I had spent the last decade working with middle school and high school students, who for the most part thought I was somewhat cool. The only reason they even remotely thought that was I was in my twenties, loved to have fun and cared about them. In other words, I was not old and thirty-something like their parents.

I remember thinking, *Old and thirty, can that even be possible? Where did the last decade go? What did I have to show for it? What had I accomplished?* Three days of questions like that can nearly make a man insane. Let's just say it did not help to stop in Graceland and see all Elvis Presley did by the time he was thirty.

Not to mention the fact that life after thirty for Elvis was not that wonderful either.

The startling reality for most young pastors is the realization that Jesus didn't even begin his earthly ministry until he was thirty. I started at twenty. That interesting parallel gave me comfort for about a minute or two (I can be a cynic at times).

Here's why the comfort dissipated. Jesus was a carpenter, or more likely a general contractor, for a large portion of his life. The Savior we know and love spent a decade plus building things with his hands. The one who long ago formed the universe out of nothing was employed on earth to construct physical structures, places one could point to or stand in.

What had I created? What was I supposed to point to? I was in full-time ministry. Should I have pointed to the programs I ran, the services I led, or the countless events I hosted? Was I supposed to point to the congregants that made up my ministry population? How do you point at people and say, "See that, I did that." We all know how well that would go over.

Speaking of full-time ministry, upon turning thirty, Jesus added that to the resume. I would think it safe to say that the three years Jesus spent in full-time ministry were, in a word, productive. He started a revolution of truth and grace. He healed blind people, cast out demons, raised people to life, and even borrowed a boy's lunch to feed five-thousand people. This renegade rabbi deeply discipled twelve no-names along with the small crowd that lingered around Him as He traveled. He confronted the systems of religious hypocrisy at every turn. He started to tear down race, gender, and social barriers in the name of the Kingdom of Heaven.

All the evidence I have points to the fact that Jesus was definitely more productive in His three years of full-time ministry than the entire ten years I had completed on my thirtieth birthday.

Additionally, places of halted spiritual transformation plagued me. At thirty I had been in ministry for a decade, but I had been following Christ for over two decades. Twenty-four years of my life had been spent in a relationship with Jesus. Yet, there were still major self-positioned roadblocks on my path toward spiritual maturity. Additionally, my final two years of ministry in Georgia had left me deeply cynical, untrusting, and very soul dry.

The cycles of sin and shame I often leaned on to cope with these feelings were not godly nor life-giving. I gained and lost weight over and over, in part due to my food addiction. I developed lazy, habitual behaviors. I worked hard for God to appease my guilt. I sought intimacy from sources that could never satisfy. My soul was an internal mess. Oh, and did I mention I was driving across the country to lead a thriving ministry at a growing church?

I knew I needed a mentor. I needed a Yoda. I craved someone who would look at me and say, "The force is strong with you, my friend." I wanted a man to teach me how to break free from my shame and experience God's love. I hoped California would be a fresh new start. Deep down, despite my internal doubts and worries, I knew God was sending me to the desert valley of Modesto for a reason. Little did I know exactly what He had in store.

Not the Answer I Was Looking For

During my first week on the job at my new church, I discovered Tuesdays were infamous for meetings. I guess this reality is true in most larger church settings in one way or another, but this church staff really liked to cram every and any possible meeting into one day. This did not sit too well with me, but mostly because I completely despise long and often pointless organizational style meetings. My general rule has always been, email the details and let's talk over a meal about life.

The college and young adult ministry which I led was partnered with the student ministry team. As a team, we would begin the day meeting to discuss ministry events and calendar items. That time was followed by an all-staff prayer gathering. Once a month we would have an all-staff lunch hour. After lunch was the all-pastors staff meeting. Finally, we would meet in pockets after the pastors meetings to decide what really needed to be done that week, and moan a little (okay, a lot) about the meeting schedule. Sounds like fun, does it not?

I won't forget what happened in the conference room during one of those first Tuesdays. It was announced that a pastor of Discipling and Spiritual Growth was going to be joining our team. His name was Jon Byron. Well, since discipling is something that I am extremely passionate about, I was interested. The senior pastor went on to explain what this new role would look like at the church and a bit more about his relationship with Jon. There was nothing but high praise spoken about him. Jokingly, one of the worship staff guys chimed in and said, "Basically, Jon is our Yoda." Now that caught my attention.

Not long after Jon arrived from Southern California, I went to visit him in his office. My intentions were clear, I was going to ask him to mentor me. I had never been so bold as to just ask someone before, but I had never been so determined or desperate either. I remember his office was not even fully unpacked and an odd assortment of furniture littered the room. He had guitar cases in one corner, as he was quite the singer, songwriter as well. The bookshelves that lined one whole wall of the office were completely packed with Jon's books, as compared to my two or three shelves of books. I figured if he had read only half of them then he would have a lot to teach me.

I quickly realized that Jon was a very unassuming man. There was not a boisterous, knowledge-based, church-conference confidence about him. Instead, there was a true sense of depth and wisdom. He had a resume that would impress many, but it was not until months and even years later that I learned of it all. He was not one to brag about his past with big stories and name-dropping.

Jon is one of those men who reminds me of Jesus in that when he is with you, you feel as though he is fully focused on you. His mind never seemed to be wandering off to what was next, or to his phone, or an email. He was attuned to you, much as I imagine Jesus would be. It also helped that Jon had a Jesus-like beard and that traditional "I am a Presbyterian bishop" look about him. If anything it made him look even more the part of a worthy mentor.

After a few pleasantries and small talk about our respective relocating adventures, I launched into my speech. I explained that I had always wanted a mentor. I shared how I heard about his capabilities and experience in mentoring people. I believe I even told him that people call him the Yoda of our church staff, which might have been too much. Then I dropped the question: "Would it be possible for you to mentor me?" After a brief pause, he spoke up.

He started off saying that he was flattered and quickly moved on to say that a few others guys had approached him about the same idea. I remember feeling immediately disappointed. I had been too late. Previous mentoring situations I had witnessed from afar caused me to think now Jon did not have time for me. He would have to invest in the one or two guys ahead of me on the list. Inside I was already back-pedaling. I remember thinking, "Maybe there would be another possible mentor, somewhere."

It was then that Jon said something strange. He told me he had told the other guys on staff the same thing. He went on to say that he did not really mentor people in the one-on-one sense. Instead, he liked to spend time in a group. My hope lifted a little as he then explained he was considering hosting a Thursday morning get-together, before work, for staff guys. During this hour, he said we would read a passage of scripture and spend time in prayer together.

Let's just say his answer was not quite what I expected him to say, not in the least.

To be honest, after his description was given, my hope fluttered away. Don't get me wrong, I love the scriptures. Of course, I am not opposed to prayer either. Despite my over-sensitive lack of trust, I really liked all of the staff guys I had met. However, I did not want just another group Bible study and prayer request hour. This was not the answer I was looking for. I wanted a Yoda. I wanted Jon to look at me and say "Yes" to my request, and mine alone. I wanted him to turn me into a Jedi for Jesus. Rather, I got invited to yet another Bible Study and a prayer time.

I am sure right now you are thinking I am a pretty horrible person, but before you judge me too harshly, hear me out. I left his office agreeing to attend the Thursday meeting, mostly out of a sense of obligation. When the time arrived I found myself in his office with four other staff members sitting on Jon's retro furniture. For an hour we spent time in the Scriptures, prayed, and shared what we individually heard from the text. That may sound fairly simple and very familiar. However, that day was anything but familiar. Something strange and unique took place that day. Maybe Jon was a Yoda after all.

QUESTIONS TO PONDER

How were you discipled after your profession of faith in Christ? Who is mentoring you now?

Have you ever attempted to be a spiritual mentor to someone else? What did you do that was successful? What might you have done differently?

Read Titus 2 and 1 Peter 5. What do these texts teach you about mentoring and discipling others who are just behind you in the journey of faith?

Have there been opportunities in your spiritual life that you said no to because they did not seem to be the answer you were looking for?

- 4 -
THE DAY THINGS CHANGED

Let the word of Christ dwell in you richly, teaching
and admonishing one another in all wisdom, singing
psalms and hymns and spiritual songs, with thankfulness
in your hearts to God. ~ *Colossians 3:16 ESV*

"We must allow the Word of God to confront us,
to disturb our security, to undermine our complacency and to
overthrow our patterns of thought and behavior." ~ *John R.W. Stott*

As we began the hour of prayer and Bible Study together that day, Jon explained what exactly we would be doing. He stated this exercise would be a practice in the art of listening. In fact, the practice we were about to participate in was adapted from Saint Augustine and sixth-century Benedictine monks. As a person who enjoys history and vintage ideas, this perked my curiosity.

The practice itself incorporated prayer, scripture, meditation, and contemplation together. Jon called it *Lectio Divina* (which in Latin means "Divine Listening").[1] Growing up Southern Baptist, this whole idea sounded a little edgy, but I chalked it up to living in California and went along for the ride.

For the record, I am not the world's greatest listener. Even when people directly say, "Now listen up!" I struggle to stay focused. So, because the framework of the hour was focused predominately on listening, I started to doubt this would even be a beneficial experience for me. Either way, I was there and figured I would give it my best shot.

He went on to share that we would follow a liturgy. We would speak a few Scriptures aloud together, and then leave silent space for prayer and reflection. I had grown up doing responsive readings

---

[1] If you google Lectio Divina, you will find a host of blog posts berating the practice as evil or mystical. Please know that I have taken the time to research and vet this specific practice immensely. What I have concluded is reading the Bible and praying for God's voice to be heard is truly revolutionary, not heretical, wayward or mystical.

at church so reading aloud together was not strange. The quiet moments of prayer and reflection seemed easy enough. I was already spending regular quiet times in my office at the start of my day, preparing for the schedule ahead. If that was the extent of the liturgy, then I knew I would be fine. *That shouldn't weird me out or confuse me,* I thought. However, Jon's next statements made me think a bit more.

He spoke about how for the first few hundred years of the church, there was no Bible. That is not to say there were not copies of the Scriptures, but they were not collected into the fixed, leather-bound formats we have today. People did not have multiple copies of the sacred texts laying around their homes like so many of us do today. Additionally, literacy was not a high cultural priority in the early days of the church. Therefore, parishioners or church members had to listen carefully to the Word of God being read aloud by the priest or leader of the church.

Before you pity the ancients and decide we have evolved greatly in our methods of church, let's perform some honest introspection. In some ways, church life is not really all that different today. I personally find it sad to see that the number of paper copies of the Scriptures fading in many of today's churches. At best they have been replaced by personal handheld devices or tablets, at worst the worship center's video screen. Video screens and Bible apps make it so we do not have to crack open the Scriptures to search out the words of Jesus together.

Our efforts to make the unchurched worship experience so comfortable have in some way created a similar quandry.

I have even heard many a church leader go as far as to say, "Don't worry about opening your Bible. Today's text will be on the screen." Unfortunately, what they do not normally say is that the passage is cut from its context so it can align all the more with the current sermon series title.

Why is it that we do not ask people to read scripture themselves and ponder it before we tell them what it means? We don't even invite people to flip through Bible pages until they find a passage themselves (or at least encourage the table of contents be their guide so the education of scripture navigation gets passed on a little). Are we robbing people of an opportunity to absorb truth with their hearts and ears? Maybe we have stepped so far into a technological time that we are actually returning to the illiteracy days of the first few centuries. Maybe even today, people depend all too much on church leadership to read the Bible to them. Either way, back to the story.

As the four other staff members and myself sat there, we had little idea how powerfully the Scriptures were going to penetrate our hearts that morning. Each of us apprehensively plodded through the liturgical pieces together, allowing God to do His work.

One of the lines of the liturgy had been taken John 6:68. It read:

To whom shall we go? You have the words of eternal life,
and we have believed and have come to know
that You are the Holy One of God.

The period of silence that followed the choral reading of this passage surprised me. I felt as though I had just spoken those very words to Jesus. I know that was the intention of the reading, but let us be honest. At times, our focus can be off-target during rote recitation. However, on this day I was keenly aware of the presence of Jesus with us; as Lord, as Rabbi, as friend. I cannot tell you how many times I have come to the Scriptures before this moment and not sensed the Lord's presence. Yet that day was different. God was sticking to us in that place like moisture on a humid Southern summer day. His presence was thick among us.

No Pressure: A Word of Phrase

Jon shared that he would be reading a gospel selection, the same passage three times. During his first reading of the text, we were invited to simply rest and listen to the words being read or follow along in our paper-copy Bibles. We were not striving to discover some miraculous new insight. We were not attempting to figure out the main theme of the text, jot down Greek words we noticed, or ponder any theological implications for the church. We were simply asked to open the ears of our heart and listen. See the ears hear, but the heart listens. We were simply asked to listen.

After Jon read, he gave us a space of nearly five minutes to sit, reflect, and even journal concerning the word or phrase we had heard. This is where my western educational upbringing kicked in. Let me explain.

Think back to your school days. Whenever a teacher asked a question like, "The President of the United States during the Civil War that pressed for the emancipation of all slaves was...," the expected result was for someone to quickly answer "Abraham Lincoln." There was no space of ten seconds, let alone five minutes, given to reflect on the name or person of Abraham Lincoln. Educational quizzing is simply question, answer, next question.

We live in a culture of immediacy as well, which does not help the process. When was the last time, during a Sunday School class or Small Group, that five minutes of silence was given for reflection? Now, I would venture to say that if your experiences with church have been anything like mine then silent space is nearly non-existent in those environments. We are so quick to fill the space with our own voices our own thoughts, or let our minds wander off to what is next that space created for Jesus to make Himself known is a rare commodity.

Why is that? Do we really believe that our thoughts are that great? You might want to reflect on that before you answer. I am being intentionally sarcastic to make a point. We love the sound of our own voices and even the voices of the famous. However, how often do we stop long enough to hear and enjoy the voice of the eternally famous one, Jesus Christ?

With that as a backdrop, my thoughts about a selected word or phrase from scripture should always pale in comparison to what Jesus wants to say. Surely I can listen for five minutes.

*For my thoughts are not your thoughts, neither are
your ways my ways, declares the Lord.* ~ Isaiah 55:8 ESV

To be honest, sitting for five minutes thinking on one word or phrase from the Scriptures takes concentration. I have a mind that is prone to wander. If you grew up in church, you are most likely proving my point right now. In your head you are probably singing the song, "Come Thou Fount" and the lines of the final verse that read: "prone to wander, prone to leave the God I love."

It is just human nature to be distracted. I invited you to think about concentrating on God's word and you may have started singing a hymn in your head. You may even be thinking that it has been ages since you last sang that song at church. Are you now thinking "Rock of Ages, cleft for me?" If so, do not be too critical of yourself. This was a trap. It was intended. Okay, back on topic now.

You can guess that developing the discipline to sit patiently in silent reflection may take time, longer than five minutes even. Just to be clear, reflection is not equal to study. Reflection is an attentiveness to the Word, not only for knowledge to be gleaned but for the person of God to be revealed. We are learning to be attentive to the presence of Jesus as the Living Word. Then and only then can one truly understand the words or phrases one finds in scripture.

After Jon read the text and a few silent moments passed, he then asked what words or phrases caught our attention. The sharing was refreshing. There was not any pressure to perform or have the right answer. Instead, the moment was centered on being in tune with what God wanted to speak to us individually.

We went around the circle and shared the different words or phrases we heard. There was no commentary added, nothing extra. Each one of us, with a sense of authority and awe, verbalized the Word of God for the whole group to hear. The phrases hung in the air of Jon's office and resonated with a peculiar sense of declaration and power. God was with us.

I Am Getting Emotional

During *Lectio Divina*'s second reading of the gospel story, we were asked to connect with our emotions as the text was read. I remember Jon mentioned we might even use our imaginations as we listened; that it might be helpful to picture ourselves in the scripture narrative. He then encouraged us to entertain the following questions:

How would we have felt if we were characters in the story?

What emotions would have bubbled to the surface?

Did we feel guilt and shame, joy and release, love and acceptance?

On the tail end of this instructional piece about how we were to listen, Jon mentioned people have the most difficulty with this type of listening. His statement was true of me as well.

Now I did not struggle with the imagination part. I have always had an active imagination. In fact, I would say that I could even give Walter Mitty a run for his money. People have called me creative at times, but I just think it is because my brain is always swimming in story, whether fiction or reality. In the extremely rare cases that I struggle to fall asleep, I make up stories in my head until I slip off to dreamland. My dreams are flooded with the semi-lucid attempts of creating and directing grand stories. People watching, in almost any public place, is a blast for me simply for the new fodder I gain for my imagination. I picture the lives of the people I watch and then build their backstories. Of course, my backstories for people are probably way more dramatic or romantic than their current situations, but one can never be too sure.

Therefore, imagining the Scriptures in my mind was not a stretch. St. Ignatius was known for encouraging imaginative prayer and meditation. He taught his followers to imagine the incarnation. In other words, people were asked to picture what Jesus sees, both positive and negative, when He looks over the world He has created. He encouraged believers to have an imaginative mind when it comes to examining the Scriptures, placing themselves inside the action of a gospel account. Ignatius felt that it released us to see the Lord in a new and fresh way, directed by the Holy Spirit.

In an interview, Eugene Peterson, one of my favorite disciple-minded authors, mentioned that William Blake always capitalized the letter "I" in imagination. It served to remind him that Holy Spirit is the one that breathes the creative and imaginative in us. I found myself intrigued by that idea and have since loved reading the Scriptures with my imagination on high. It breathes life into the text. It brings out new depth and dimension. It wows me with mystery and it even surprises me with humor.

The part of Jon's invitation that I wrestled with specifically was the emotional piece. You have to remember that I grew up in a denomination that was, at best, leery of human emotion. I remember being taught that we could trust cold hard facts but feelings were definitely suspect. I recall comparing this concept to the scene in Star Wars

Emotions are not the culprit of sin, however, our reactions can be. Jesus wants to redeem every part of us, emotions included.

when the Emperor is provoking Luke to search out and trust his feelings, but deep down we know it to be a bad decision for the young Jedi. Sure, that is a silly example, but my thoughts about emotional trust have always been laced with similar doubts.

The popular Campus Crusade teaching of this idea was illustrated as a train. The locomotive's engine was labeled *FACT*. The train's single car was called *FAITH*. Finally, the caboose was titled *FEELINGS*.

Now I fully understand the intention of the diagram as a tool to show that our faith is built on solid ground. But no matter how true the moniker is, I found it very confusing. Surely I was not intended to be the Christian version of Spock. Or was I?

Didn't Jesus have feelings? Didn't He get upset at the money changers in the temple, the stubbornness of His own disciples, and even an out-of-season fig tree? Didn't He feel deep compassion toward the helpless, weep in grief at Lazarus' tomb and cry out in anguish of heart in Gethsemane? Those are real, raw emotions the last time I checked.

Additionally, according to every sound theology lesson I have ever had, Jesus was fully human in every way. If that is true, a *fact* one might even say, then should I have the right to embrace my emotions as Jesus did? The truth is I can, we can. It is just that we must do so *without* sinning, as did our Lord and Savior.

It may feel strange to think that we could be angry but not sin or be over-joyed and not drift toward selfishness, and yet it's possible. Emotions must be felt, examined, and channeled into holiness. I believe we have been more than subtly taught to steer clear of our emotional side as it is more a symptom of our sin nature than a holistic part of our on-going redemption. However, this is just not true.

As Jon read the gospel text, I remember struggling to let myself identify personally with an emotion. I could empathize with the obvious and assumed feelings of the people in the text. But for me, as an individual, it was difficult to pinpoint how I truly felt. When the time came for us to share our emotional connection with the text, I stumbled through that day's attempt.

In the weeks that followed, my sensitivity to the emotional side of my soul reached new heights. That which I had at one time tried to repress or contain among churched people was now an undiscovered box of treasure found in the attic. I began learning how to explore my thoughts, character, and emotions in a healthy way. I was learning how to be me, the unique person that Jesus had made of me. It was different, but it also felt very joyful.

An Invitation from Jesus

Before our third and final reading of the same text, Jon coached us to listen for a personal invitation Jesus would have for us that day. The invitation itself was to be a sentence or two we could state in such a way that it felt like Jesus was speaking it Himself. It was made clear that even more important than what the exact invitation was, our awareness of Him with us, speaking the invitation, was truly premiere. When Jon read again, we listened attentively for the calling of Jesus that day.

The reading was followed, yet one more time, with a moment of silent reflection. Honestly, it felt odd to read a passage three times and then ask only one question per reading. Why not just read the text once and ask three questions? That is what I was familiar with. Would that not be a more efficient use of time?

Every Bible study, small group experience, or even seminary class I'd ever been in was designed that way. If a text was read, the leader would read it once and then ask their list of questions. Interesting enough, I have since noticed that our answers to these questions usually skip the emotional and personal connections.

More often than not, the answers that are given to Bible Study questions are stated in the third person as well. For example, you will hear, "The church needs to..." or "The world always..." There is rarely a moment when the answer to a question actually forces us to be openly vulnerable or authentic in public. Either that or we take the easy way out by answering in third person, which is too easily allowed by many group facilitators.

Think about it, when is the last time that someone in your church's small group shared something like this: "After reading the story of Zaccheaus, I realize I am hoarding my money and possessions." That usually does not happen. No, instead our sharing gets centered around the world's emphasis on money being overly important. It may sound something like this: "Isn't it sad that some people let money destroy them?"

I do not mean to be a critic, but answers like that leave me empty. Sometimes I get even downright frustrated. It is in those moments that I want to become like the prophet Nathan before the wayward King David and shout, "You are that man!" Or at least want to say, "I am and we are that man." A little soul-condition ownership would go a long way in creating authentic, life-transforming settings.

If there is one thing I have learned about the practice of Lectio is that it forces one to be vulnerable. It forces one to say, "This is what Jesus is saying to me right now." It pushes a money-hungry, modern-day Zaccheaus to confess his current love of currency. It forces an image-is-everything, suburban soccer-mom to say that she has made an idol of her free-time and appearance. The Pharisee-like church-goer may even be forced to confess his or her sinful judgment of the Zaccheaus' in his or her workplace. The invitational piece of *Lectio Divina* pries into the heart and forces a transforming vulnerability like none other.

It is important to note that one reason this sacred practice is successful in eliciting such openness on a deep level is that no one is encouraged to respond or comment on another's individual sharing time; whether it be word, emotion, or invitation. Statements are left hanging in the air for all to hear, consider, and appreciate. Because no one is fixed or trumped during sharing, it is the authority of Jesus' divine messages delivered to His children that saturate the moment.[2]

---

[2] Of course statements of significant heresy are politely addressed, especially since they most often stem from infant understanding and not staunch doctrinal rebellion.

The whole process is truly a rich experience. However, it is very important to note that the power is not in the process. No, instead power comes as individuals commit to hearing a loving God make Himself known to a people eager and willing to respond in obedience. It comes through a renewed belief that Jesus longs to speak to our hearts. Our Savior has words of comfort, care, and correction to share with us daily. We have ears and He was words. We have concerns and He brings clarity. We long for relational intimacy and He provides His presence. There is nothing greater than that; getting to know the One who knows us fully.

The truth is, for me, *Lectio Divina* became a training ground for listening to Jesus speak. Jon, my Yoda, knew that. He was not teaching me techniques or tricks to become a better church leader. Instead, he was helping me be a better listener which in turn would make me a better Kingdom leader.

Although it felt somewhat backward at the time, I look back on it now and realize the whole plan was ingenious. Jon was not mentoring me to be like him or to learn and retain the knowledge he had found in the books on his shelf. That seems to be what happens all too often in the typical mentoring process. However, as we all know, simply mimicking another human is not that healthy of a practice. Jon was discipling me to hear the Good Shepherd and follow Him. He knew my number one weakness was learning to listen to Jesus' voice. I had ears, but I didn't always hear.

QUESTIONS TO PONDER

Have you ever had a true discipleship-based mentor in your life?

When you read scripture, are you searching for answers to questions or are you eager to simply be in the presence of God, listening for His voice?

How do you deal with your emotions? Do you have a tendency to bottle them up? Are you more apt to share your emotions with others? Do you control them or do they tend to control you?

How did your denomination or religious upbringing teach you to handle the topic of emotions and your faith?

With what level of frequency do you feel you apply the invitations of God in your life? Great frequency? Minimal? How might Christ-like transformation be aided by your greater level of response?

- 5-
LIVING LA VIDA LECTIO

*Teach me your way, Lord, that I may rely on your faithfulness; give
me an undivided heart, that I may fear your name. ~ Psalm 86:11 NIV*

*"I must take care above all that I cultivate communion
with Christ, for though that can never be the basis of my peace...
it will be the channel of it." ~ Charles H. Spurgeon*

Since that first day with Jon and my fellow staff members, the practice of *Lectio Divina* has steadily woven itself into the fabric of my lifestyle. That hour a week with Jon, the guys, and the scripture was wonderful. However, I think we would all agree that listening to God speak is too valuable to limit to an hour a day, one time a week with a select group of friends. If God's voice can be heard at all times, then I want to— no, I need to— be attentive every waking and sleeping, moment. That level of attentiveness is an ambitious goal I know, but why would I settle for anything less?

I can get slightly weirded out when I stop to think about all the radio station frequencies, microwaves, Wi-Fi and mobile phone transmissions that are taking place around me all the time. Tons of useless data is endlessly swirling about me daily. However, to know that God desires to reveal Himself to me continually is astounding. Dialing into these divine transmissions demands a lifestyle of *Lectio Divina* (divine listening), or as no one south of the border calls it: Living La Vida Lectio.

Now before you think I am about to advocate for monastic living like the Benedictine priests that made the practice common, I am not. I am not asking you to become a monk, a nun or even cloister yourself up for years until you master the fine art of listening. I would venture to say that even if you asked a life-long monk if he has mastered the art of listening to God he would probably be quick to say that he has just begun to scratch the surface.

Of course, there are a plethora of methods that can aid in one's learning to listen to God. There are retreat experiences, studies on the early church practices, and countless spiritual disciplines one might employ. For the remainder of this chapter, I hope to introduce you to a few simple tools I have found helpful in my quest to master the fine art of listening. I trust they will be a blessing to you as well.

Sticks, Stars, and Signs

The primary tool is what I like to call *Sticks, Stars, and Signs*. It is birthed directly out of my practice of *Lectio Divina*. But it has become a framework for so much more in my life, as you will see throughout the remainder of the book. The simplicity of *Sticks, Stars, and Signs* has helped me personally engage with the God of the Scriptures versus just consuming the various facts of a holy book. Our God is more than the Wikipedia page about Him. If the Scriptures are truly living and active, then I want to meet that living God and know His activity in my life. I would assume if you are reading this book, that is true of you as well. *Sticks, Stars, and Signs* keeps that focus before me.

Sticks

Growing up in a small town left little to do in the way of entertainment. Plus I didn't grow up with the internet, email, or even cable television. Now cable television was around, but not for our family. My parents would tell my brother, sister, and I to go play outside, read a book, "go do something." The idea of technological entertainment which people have access to today was not even an option when I was a kid. So what did we do? Well, we made up games in the yard and rode our bikes everywhere.

I remember one day some friends and I pedaled down a gravel road that led out of town. Trips outside of town on the bike were not exactly encouraged, but they were an adventure. About a half mile into our trip we came upon a thicket of trees by a small creek. The cluster of trees, we were surprised to find, had become a salvage dump of sorts. It was filled with old washing machines, couches, luggage, and you name it. Now that I think about it, that ditch of discovery also probably contained a good bit of tetanus, too. But what did we care? We lived on the wild side back then.

The afternoon was spent rummaging through the abandoned pile of junk. There was one item that stuck out, literally, during our digging. While rummaging around that day, I caught myself on a piece of barbwire fencing. The jagged wire grabbed my leg and cut me deep enough to draw blood. To some people that is not a big deal, but if you know me at all you know that I am a complete wimp when it comes to blood. I know it is all a psychological weakness and maybe one day I will be delivered. However, it has not happened yet. Needless to say, of all the items we combed through that day, the item I remember most was the barbwire.

In a strangely similar way, this story applies to my lifestyle of learning to listen. When I read the Scriptures, I slowly read through the text until something sticks out to me; a word or phrase specifically. I then spend time reflecting on why that particular phrase jumped out. During my time of reflection, I question why God might be drawing my attention toward that word or phrase. I think about what is happening in my life that makes that exact word or phrase pierce my heart more than any other.

That is the joy of having an all-knowing God. I so not have to search relentlessly for a hidden truth when He delivers what I need each day.

The various Bibles I have used over the years are filled with underlined words or phrases. My devotional journals are underscored, literally, by the words God would have for me that day. My meditations on scripture are always about what has stuck out to me that day. Without fail, God always highlights the right words for the right reason at the right season of my life.

Stars

During the summer of 2009, I had the opportunity to explore some of the Northern California backcountries. Darrell, a friend from church, had set up a four-day camping trip to a place called Kennedy Meadows. Without a doubt, this meadow is one of the most pristine and beautiful places I have ever been. The trip was made up of five men hiking into the wilderness for just under a week.

The trip reminded me a little of the Oregon Trail game I had played as a kid, just with better graphics and we did not have to kill a bear or ford a river (Plus no one died of cholera. Now that I think about it, that game was an odd way to introduce kids to the historical dangers of westward expansion). Before the four days were up, I had had one of my most memorable experiences ever, especially for a city boy like myself.

The meadow was located about a mile above sea level, so the air was thin and clean. To get to the prime camping spot that Darrell and his family had enjoyed summer's before meant hiking five plus miles from where we parked our truck. Overall the individual hike was not too bad. The most difficult part was the first few miles, which rose upward sharply and winded through a fairly rocky terrain. I remember my heavy breathing and the thin mountain air not being the best combo.

Thankfully all our supplies were hauled in by mule. That was quite a sight to see. Four mules backs packed to the brim, marching steadily up the mountain face following the trail boss on his horse. Watching the trail boss and the mules navigate the rocky landscape I could not tell if they or I were working harder. It made me imagine what it must have been like to cross these mountains for the first time in search for the Western seaboard. It was then that I thanked God for being born when I was. Did I mention that I grew up in town?

After the mules were unloaded, firewood was gathered, and camp was set up, we ate dinner. Now for all of the people who think of camping food to be basic and boring, well then you need to meet Darrell. This man can make some amazing feasts on an open flame. We ate like the kings of that mountain meadow for four days.

With bellies full each night, we sat around the campfire and told stories, laughing late into the night. With no streetlights around, night was truly dark. In fact, it was so dark I hesitated to walk off too far to use the bathroom for fear that some wild animal lurking in the bushes might jump out and grab me, and I would never see it coming. My flashlight dependency grew strong that week; that was until I made a startling discovery. I looked up.

That may seem like a silly thing to say, but in the city, you do not look up that much. There is nothing to see. The Only thing *up* in the city is a distant airplane flashing by, an occasional hospital helicopter, or maybe the moon. However, the night sky in Kennedy

Meadows is nothing short of spectacular. I have never seen so many stars, and so vivid. I recall asking why the sky seemed cloudy and star-filled at the same time. I was told that what I was seeing was the Milky Way and if I watched carefully I would see the occasional satellite go streaming by.

I don't know about you, or how you would have reacted to this moment of sudden wonder at the immense visibility of the galaxy in which we live, but I was awed. I sat quietly and just stared for quite some time. Maybe it was the crackling fire, the full stomach, and the view all together that overwhelmed me. All I know is that I found myself extremely emotional.

I was moved by a God that created all that my eyes could perceive, in addition to everything my eye could not or never would see. I was dumbfounded by the beauty. I was humbled by the sheer immensity of the mountains, the meadow, the sky, and the greater expanse of the galaxy in comparison to the minuscule collection of dust that was me. Laying there on my cot, I fought back tears that night. Seriously though, I *had* to fight back tears. It was a guy's weekend and I did not want to be too sensitive.

This experience translates perfectly into my everyday reading of the word. If I can become an emotional mess looking at a mountain and the night sky, then surely the Scriptures should move me. Surely God's voice should elicit a deeply emotional response. Whether it be tears, anger, conviction, or joy, there ought to be some reaction from my soul, a soul which longs to live connected to God.

Why is it that we can be so in touch with our emotions in the everyday moments of life, but when faced with our feelings concerning the sacred we clam up?

It is somewhat startling to me how tricky this emotional piece is for myself and others. Often when someone is asked to articulate how the scriptures move us personally, there is little to no direct connection. Oh, we can regurgitate the basic talking points of the narrative, usually something gleaned from the teaching of a favorite celebrity pastor. We might even mention something of the context or a stray correlation to another piece of scripture. However, clarifying how we sincerely *feel in light of the reading of God's word can seem almost foreign.* I find this phenomenon strange considering we know exactly how we feel about bad drivers, long lines at the grocery store, or horrible service at our favorite restaurant.

Though the question continues to stump me, my best guess is that we are uncomfortable being emotional before God. Somehow we have come to believe we are to be docile, robotic beings in servitude to the Lord without the slightest sign of real emotion; that is unless it is the exuberant joy of worship or the phony Pharisaic smile. We were made human, in the image of God. Last I checked that means we get to express our emotions just as He did, only without sin.

Let's Take An Emotions Test

How does it make you feel that Jesus wept at Lazarus' tomb?

*How does it make you feel that King David
put a hit out on Uriah, his mistress' husband?*

*How does it make you feel that John the Baptist was
murdered because a government official got drunk and wanted
to impress his friends with the naked dancing of his stepdaughter?*

I can tell you exactly how these scriptural moments make me feel. I feel confused and saddened at Jesus weeping. I feel disgusted at David, and without a doubt, I feel sickened and enraged at the story of John's untimely end.

The Scriptures are meant to move us. They were written to convict and inspire us. The challenges they deliver are meant to compel us to love and good deeds. All that we read in the Bible is meant to come alive in our hearts and flood us with joy, purpose, and mission. If you are missing the emotional connection with God's word, then you will miss the joy that comes with His purpose and mission for you.

I like to draw an actual star in my journal and write down the emotions I feel in the passages of scripture I read. The symbol serves as a Kennedy Meadows reminder that I am to be awed and moved by the Savior and His messages of love and hope aimed at my heart.

An interesting truth about the emotional piece of *Sticks, Stars, and Signs* is often times the feelings I discover as I listen to the text are the same feelings I am wrestling through in other places of my life. Personally, I don't find the parallel a coincidence. I believe is it the Holy Spirit coaching me on how I might properly process my emotional connections in order to better glorify the Father.

Signs

I am not a guy who likes to be lost. I should explain that a little better because I haven't met many people who enjoy being lost. I don't like to drive somewhere without solid directions in hand. The invention of turn-by-turn directions sent to your phone and vocalized for you to hear was made for people just like me. Nothing about me wants to wander in the *somewhat* right direction. No, I want to get there, and quick. I know I am not like most men in that way. I will always stop for directions. I want to know exactly where I am going at all times.

The same is true in my life as a whole. I do not want to wander around aimlessly searching for purpose or direction. I want it given to me clear and quick. Sadly, if we do not believe our Heavenly Father wants to deliver His directions to us, we will allow others to shape and determine the route for us.

I cannot tell you how many college students I have counseled that are pursuing a career solely because it was the path painted and pushed by their parents, or in direct rebellion to the same path. As godly as parental guides in our life can be, that is not whom you ultimately want charting a child's career course.

For those who desire life-long companionship with a spouse, do you, or did you, pursue relationships and endure the dangers of dating, courting? Of course, you did. That is the direction you must take if you want to meet someone, fall in love, and begin a life together. If you never take the great risk to love another, then marriage will never happen.

There is so much in life that only happens when we follow the signs, listen for directions or commit to a pathway of discipline. How many goals are ever reached in life by the aimless? How many children have been adopted accidentally? How many wars are started without a greater intention? The answer is none. Goals take direction. Redeeming the sanctity of broken families through adoption takes purpose. Going to battle is the outcome of choosing a path of pain in hopes of a greater peace.

When Jesus left heaven, He had a goal. He came to be the Savior of the world, reconciling all people to the Father. When Jesus became human He had a family in mind. His purpose was that we would all become true sons and daughters of the Most High God, adopted into His eternal family. Our Christ did not arrive on the planet and not expect a battle. His painful war with the prince of darkness via the cross and the resurrection is the reason we can even know peace in our hearts today. That was His direction. That was His pathway. He followed the signs.

It only makes sense that when we read the Scriptures that we hear in them a sense of purpose and direction for our lives too. I trust that you see the signposts written in God's word, pointing you to peace with Him. I hope you see the warning signs, placed along the way to divert you from destruction. I pray you see the trail markers that beg you to venture down a path less traveled. I want for everyone that the Scriptures would declare the gracious and glorious invitations of our God and King.

When Jesus left His throne in heaven, He had a goal. He followed the signs the Father had given Him.

The listening tool of *Sticks, Stars, and Signs* is only complete when we hear the voice of the Lord inviting us to take the next step with Him. As I engage God in devotion daily, I ask myself, "What is the sign or invitation you have for me today Lord?" Often times the step I must take is one toward greater intimacy with Him. Some days the invitation is to deeper confession, repentance, and brokenness over my selfish nature. Without fail, the signs are always pointing to the Great Commission. Jesus is always reminding me that I am in a battle with Him for the hearts of His wayward sons and daughters. I just need to watch for the signs.

I hope you are hearing the invitations of God in your life. If you do, I trust you are writing them down, praying over them, and sharing them with others. Writing them down helps them be remembered and subsequently acted on. The more public your invitations become, the more accountability you will have and the more likely your invitations will be obeyed.

Listening Beyond the Bible

Earlier I mentioned the activity of scripture reading as a key method of listening to God. I believe in that method because that is where one must begin. The truth is that we have to become familiar with how God spoke and interacted with others. As believers, we need to gain a foundational knowledge of what God is about; His nature, His character on display. It's through the Bible that we discover what our God is for and what He is against. The Bible offers an abundance of examples of people hearing and responding to God's voice. The Scriptures are definitely the place to begin listening to God and a place to practice *Sticks, Stars, and Signs*.

However, to truly make listening a lifestyle, one has to learn to recognize the voice of God even when you are not holding a copy of the Scriptures. Be careful how you hear what I am saying. I am not arguing that there is something even more important than scripture. I am simply implying that until you get used to hearing God's voice in His Word, you won't notice it elsewhere. Let's now walk through a few ways that listening, recognizing God's voice in the everyday moments, can become a true lifestyle.

Marvelously Mundane

Do you ever struggle with everyday routines and the mundaneness they bring? I have, at times, done basic assembly line work, and I have hated it. There is no way that I could, for my main income, do assembly line work for the rest of my life. I would go crazy in a short period of time due to the dull repetition.

If we are honest, life can get to feeling like a dull repetitive cycle. As much as we desire for God to wow us with an angel or some other miraculous sign that validates the direction of our life, it could be in the most simple of routines that we will really begin to hear God speak.

He anticipated God's arrival and God's voice even in the mundane.

Brother Lawrence was a lay Carmelite monk from the mid-1600s that worked in a kitchen of a monastery. He was known for having such a deep intimacy with Christ and a profound sense of peace about him that people would write letters to him for counsel.

It has been said that even the Pope stopped in his kitchen to talk about life and Lawrence's holy connection with God.

There was nothing glamorous about Brother Lawrence's daily routines that drew a crowd for counsel. Yet, over the chopping of vegetables and the baking of bread, God would speak to the heart of this simple man. The key was that Brother Lawrence was expecting the Lord to show up.

After following Jesus for over thirty-two years now, I can tell you searching for God in only the astonishing robs you from witnessing the marvelous in the mundane. As Brother Lawrence would argue in his letters, it is the practice of noticing the presence and the voice of God in the simplest of moments that must capture your heart.

Think about your upcoming schedule this week...

What are those mundane routines you have ahead of you?

When might you be driving alone?

Could that commute be the best opportunity
for you to speak with God that day?

What about when you are cleaning the house?

How can your most mundane activities be the most redemptive ones?

How might you tune-in to the Lord in those places?

How might you see the marvelous work
God desires to do in your heart?

Be careful to understand that I am not arguing for you to fill the silence with the noise of Christian sub-culture music, radio, or a celebrity pastor preaching. I am asking you to let God come alongside you in the quiet and simplicity and speak profoundly to your ears. You have ears, but will you hear— even in the mundane minutia of life?

Metaphorically Challenged

I believe that another listening tool in a Christ-follower's tool belt is that of the metaphor. Metaphors are my favorite. I love their use of imagery, storytelling, and real life connections. I especially love when business logos become a visual metaphor for what service they provide. FedEx is the perfect example. The first time I realized there was an arrow between the letters "E" and "x" I was literally excited. That is spot on! FedEx is the arrow line. Your package starts with them and gets to you. It is the beauty of a metaphor to communicate truth so simply.

I find many people do not understand the role metaphors can play in helping us better see the work of God. Jokingly, I call these people metaphorically challenged. You may or may not be one. I don't judge. Just join the ranks of Nicodemus in John 3 (go read it). Metaphorical parallels are just too deliberate for us not to realize God wants to use them powerfully in our lives.

I see metaphors everywhere, whether it is in everyday life events, movies I watch, or even in the word pictures of song lyrics. God is always speaking to me in the midst of those mediums saying "this" is like "that." If I am moved by a movie scene where a father demonstrates love to his son, the metaphoric parallel is I love when God the Father tells me, "You are my beloved son in whom I am well pleased." When I find myself impatient with the lack of attention a store employee is giving me, Jesus uses that metaphorical moment to shout in my ear: "This is not your world. Quit being so selfish and acting like it all revolves around you." Unfortunately, this lesson is one I have to learn over and over.

Mastering the art of hearing God in metaphors is like getting the chance to hear Jesus teach a parable for the very first time.

For some of you, this style of listening may prove difficult. However, it just takes practice. Try an experiment this week. In the *Questions to Ponder* section at the end of this chapter, engage in the metaphor practices. I trust that God will use metaphors to open your heart and mind to what He wants to do in and through your life.

Make Space for Him and God Will Show Up

If we continue to take the time needed to sharpen our listening skills, God will make Himself known. If we continue to make space for God to dwell in us, He will fill that space. That is the beauty of the creation account in the first chapter of Genesis.

What has always stuck out to me in the creation story is the phrase about the earth being "without form and void" in the second verse. From that one verse spills the rest of the chapter, which is the story of how God formed the world, gave it structure and limits, and then filled it. He gave the sun and moon to separate day and night and decorate the skies. To the air God gave birds, and to the seas God gave fish. Finally, He filled the land with plants, animals, and ultimately humans, His people. Everything that was once empty was filled by God.

In the same way, if we intentionally give structure and space to our divine listening, God show up powerfully. God will forever fill us with His words, His messages, and His truth. This filling will, in turn, lead to life-long transformation. Transformation is evidence that God has filled hearts, no longer leaving us formless or void.

QUESTIONS TO PONDER

Give the tools in this chapter a try. Turn to the appendix for examples of how you may journal a Sticks, Stars, and Signs time. Select a passage of scripture and record your insights. Then make time to share those insights with a family member, friend or co-worker.

What routines might be more sanctified or holy with the mindset of listening for Jesus in the midst of even what seems mundane?

Interact with life metaphors this week by answering the following:

This day is like?   *My life is like?*
My relationship with God is like?   *My family is like?*

What are the redemptive places you have seen in movies, TV shows lately? How do those places remind you of or connect you with God?

- 6 -
OBEDIENCE MATTERS

I call heaven and earth to witness against you today, that I have set before you life and death, blessing and curse. Therefore choose life, that you and your offspring may live. ~ Deuteronomy 30:19 ESV

"The best measure of a spiritual life is not its ecstasies but its obedience." ~ Oswald Chambers

Quite a few years back my wife and I purchased a used Jeep. I was excited about it because it was our transition away from the family mini-van. No matter how cool they make mini-vans today, no man has ever felt a rush of testosterone while driving one. Plus, I had always wanted a Jeep. This moment was somewhat a dream come true.

Now the Jeep I wanted and the Jeep I purchased were decidedly different. I wanted the rugged looking Wrangler. What we got was a good-looking black Jeep Cherokee. I was willing to compromise since our new wheels came with leather seats and power everything. Not only did we get a great deal on the vehicle, but my manliness factor had risen as well. My wife liked the features, and we had room for the kiddos and a plethora of groceries, too. The only negative about the car was a glittery butterfly sticker on the front license plate tag spot. I quickly covered that up with a cheap vanity sports tag.

My manly mobile ran great for a few months. Then it began acting up. Acting up is the Shawn Stutz way of telling a mechanic, "I know nothing about cars, but I do know my car should not be doing this." The first act up moment involved the power locks. They would lock and unlock whenever they wanted while the car was running.

It was most definitely annoying to hear the locks click on and off at random while driving. Passenger friends would look at me as if I were playing with the doors. I would then explain, "No, it is just the Jeep acting up." Of course, the mechanic was little to no help. I will share more about that in a moment. Let me first tell you about the second, and more serious, snafu with the Jeep.

One day while driving at seventy miles per hour down the highway, it just turned off. I mean, the whole engine shut off. The key was turned, but the car was not running. There was no gas powering the motor, no powering steering, and no anti-lock brakes. My automobile had turned into a two-ton metal sled right in the middle of the road. I did not remember purchasing a highway sled. I needed a car.

After stopping on the side of the road and exclaiming how much I loved my car, I popped the hood and looked at the engine. I did not know what I was looking for, nor did I know how to fix anything were I to actually find a problem. But I stared at the engine in anger for a bit.

Upon returning to the driver's seat, I attempted to restart the car. Bingo. It fired up like nothing had ever happened. I cautiously drove it a few hundred yards to see if the sudden power failure would occur again. *Nothing.* It was as if the power down had never happened. Believing that God had chosen to heal my Jeep and that ignorance was bliss, I drove on. I made it to my destination and nearly the whole way home before the demon within the Jeep manifested itself again. This time, the engine growled and shook briefly before switching into third gear. It then proceeded to stay in third gear only.

Driving in the mountains of Northern Georgia in third gear is pretty ridiculous. Starting up a hill after a stop light was nearly impossible. People were flashing lights at me and honking while my Jeep grunted ever so slowly up the incline. I remembered thinking, *Well, at least my hazard lights work.* My joys over getting my manly mobile quickly vanished.

Upon taking my car to the mechanic, we discovered that there was significant damage to the electrical system. All of the solenoids that operate the processes of the car were connected in a chain. So basically, when one went bad, it would overload the system and cause other parts of the electrical chain to fail. When my locks finally failed, the engine turned off as a precaution, which is good, because who doesn't want to be locked inside a runaway metal sled.

After many trips to different mechanics and many paychecks spent on keeping our sled powered, Michelle and I quickly became acquainted with the saying: *Jeep, Just Empty Every Pocket.* In time, we decided to get a whole new vehicle.

Later that year we discovered that the Jeep had been struck by lightning. An insurance agent we knew from church told us he filed a claim, about a year prior, for a Jeep just like ours. He said he remembered it specifically because it had a glittery butterfly sticker on the front license plate tag spot. Let's just say, I was slightly more than mad upon learning this news. Of course, that fact was never revealed to us during our purchase.

However, during the whole ordeal, the most frustrating part was the options the mechanic would give me to fix the Jeep. He would say things like, "Well, you can get a new solenoid or replace the whole computer system." What?! Or the mechanic would offer this solution: "You can try replacing the transmission, or drive it in third gear only."

I remember thinking how those options covered quite a wide spectrum. Inside I wondered if he was even serious. Unfortunately, he was serious. I would grimly laugh so I would not blow a gasket (which was the only part of the car that worked), and chose the lesser of two evils. Whenever he would lay out my choices in such a drastic measure, I feel it was his way of saying, "This is what I want you to pick. Make the obvious choice."

I wonder if that is the way things often are when it comes to listening to or responding to God's voice. In Deuteronomy 30:19, Moses gives Israel a word from the Lord saying, "I call heaven and earth to witness against you today, that I have set before you life and death, blessing and curse. Therefore choose life, that you and your offspring may live" (ESV). Now I do not know about you, but the word "live" in that final sentence definitely sticks out to me.

Our obedience can take various forms. It can be simply believing what He spoke is true or it could mean God is calling you to plant a church. No matter what is said, obedience is the needed response. Yet, obedience is often the most difficult or last of the human responses.

Christian living has more to do with obedience than you may think. Anytime God speaks to us, He is inviting us to respond to Him in obedience.

When our options are laid out in such an extreme way, as a matter of life or death, how can our response be anything other than a life of obedience? Have you ever really thought about that? God has stated that what he calls life flows from us choosing to respond to Him in the affirmative. Adversely, whenever we choose to neglect or ignore His wisdom, we embrace destruction and ultimately death.

When you really stop and examine the facts, why would we choose anything other than obedience and life? It seems obvious. However, the people of God have been wrestling with this truth for quite some time now. Let's take a quick trip back to the beginning of mankind and see what I mean.

Bible Character (Dis)Obedience

Adam and Eve, the first humans on the planet, did not seem to have it all that rough. God provided their needs, the Garden was plush with plants to eat from, and God had only one real rule. He told the newlywed couple to never eat from the fruit of the tree in the center of the garden. But, as we all know, they ate the fruit. No matter what Adam and Eve may have done right, they are forever remembered as the first man and woman to disobey God. God spoke. Obedience was the desired response. Adam and Eve failed, and miserably.

Fast forward to the children of Israel encamped on the edge of the Promise Land. In so many words, God had basically said, "This is the land I have given you. I will lead you to possess it. This is why I rescued you from Eygpt, that you might be for me a peculiar people and that you may worship me in the land I give you."

Of course, the Israelite response was not the model of obedience one would hope. Instead, they formed a committee to research the problem because we all know great things happen in churches and government systems because of committees (please sense the thick layer of sarcasm). The committee returned with their findings, declaring that ten of the twelve-member research party decided the Promise Land was too dangerous to pursue. This is, of course, after God told them they had been given the land and He would fight for them. Instead, the disobedient children of Israel got to wander in the desert for forty years until most of the committee died.

Now let us skip to the New Testament, late in the gospel accounts, to when yet another vote is taking place. Pilate is giving the nation of Israel a choice, Jesus or Barabbas? As a customary favor to the Jews during Passover, Pilate basically asks the people whether or not they would like to free the author of life or a murdering revolutionary. Once again, the human race chooses death over life.

It is no wonder I am a bit hesitant of the congregational model of church where everyone gets a vote. The only two examples of this method I see in scripture both had horrible outcomes; refusing the Promise Land and voting to crucify Christ. Thankfully, as we now all know, the death of Jesus would bring us life. Yes, despite even our wretched disobedience, God has saw fit to still give us the gift of life eternal.

Life or Death

Life or Death: Which would you pick? I mean seriously, is that even a choice? Well, it seems to be a reality for all humans. Despite the obvious downside to not trusting God's word and His invitations as pathways to life, we still choose death. Why is that do you think? I would argue it has much to do with surrender.

Surrender in itself feels like death. It is relinquishing of control. It is giving up personal desire. It is releasing specific comforts even when it appears illogical. I wonder if surrender sounds so much like losing and defeat to us humans that everything in us actually fights to resist it. Maybe it is even a survival mechanism. We stubbornly do not want to give up control, but we do not want death either.

The true biblical model of surrender is a much different idea; a much more beautiful concept. Jesus taught that unless a kernel of seed falls to the ground and then dies, it cannot produce life. For many of us, the idea of willful death and surrender sounds terrifying, but hopefully, the image of dying as a seed to become a grand flower is way more appealing. We have to remember that obedience brings life only when we fully surrender our life to Christ. It is not about what is lost, but what will be gained— life.

If you are struggling, in the flesh, with obedience, then you must remember there is no struggle in true surrender.

I love the way Jesuit missionary and theology professor, Thomas Green, compares the act of surrender to that of floating in the sea. He writes, "In terms of floating... we have learned to be at home in the sea that is God, with no visible means of support except the water whose ebb and flow, whose sudden surgings, we cannot predict or control." It takes trust to release the control of our will to God. But who greater to trust than the One who sees all and knows all. May I invite you to: struggle not, surrender more, and float on.

The older I get the more astounded I am at the idea that simple obedience to God is the gateway to abundant life. When I chose to take Jesus at His word and live according to His teachings, then and only then do I experience the depth of joy I am intended to experience in my relationship with Christ. It is as if eternal life is sampled every time I choose obedience.

Think of it this way. If you race through a speed trap every day only to get an expensive ticket each time, you will soon dread driving, be broke, or both. The other alternative is to surrender to the law, not as a limit to your freedom but as a means to greater freedom and life. Obedience and surrender are not concepts designed by God to restrict us from joy. They are actually wonderful truths God has employed to bring us life and life to the fullest (John 10:10). Let us choose life, that we may live.

All Things for Good

Living obediently surrendered to Christ does not mean that we are completely exempt from the consequences of prior choices. No, the thief may still spend a season in prison for her past crime despite a present surrender to Christ. A swindler might still be forced to make restitution for his past schemes even in spite of his current condition of regular obedience to God. Choosing life today does not mean that we will not be dealing with the decay of past decisions.

I know I wrestle with this reality. For a season, I made food an idol. My god was my stomach and it was never satisfied. I always craved more food. Food was my reward, my punishment, my joy, and my pain. As you might imagine, it wasn't long before I was very overweight, out of shape, and miserable in my own skin. Until I surrendered my eating habits to the Lord, I never truly experienced freedom in this area of life.

Though I have a godly perspective on eating and the idol it can become, I still have to deal with the decay of past decisions. I have a horrible metabolism due to my past binge eating. I have the stretch marks that remind me of the days I chose food, over my Savior, for comfort. The shame of my sin plagues my self-image. Plus I still battle unhealthy spiritual temptations every day. It goes without saying that I must daily surrender and choose life.

There is good news, too. Because of the truth of scripture, I also understand that God can take all my present obedience, along with my past disobedience, and meld them together into something useful and good. Romans 8:28 teaches us "in all things God works for the good of those who love him." God has taken my sinfulness at the plate and turned it into a means to minister to others who suffer from food addictions and unhealthy food behaviors.

When I see severely overweight people, I feel a sense of deep sadness, and I want to help. I enjoy helping people lose weight and get control of their fitness level because I know the curses and death I experienced when I lived in disobedience at the dinner table. I also know the life that comes in honoring God with my body. It is sustaining life, not found in any food, and I want to share that life with everyone.

We must always remember blessings and life are found in our obedience. Curses and death are found in our disobedience. Redemption and restoration can only be found in our daily surrender to Christ. Therefore, choose life that you may live.

QUESTIONS TO PONDER

Is it more a struggle to know what God has spoken or to be obedient to that which He spoke?

What moment in your life sticks out when the choice of blessings and curses, life and death were set before you and you chose poorly? How about a time that you chose properly?

When a choice is presented so boldly in terms of life and death, why is it we even entertain disobedience and death?

How has God taken both the blessings and cursings in your life and turned them into something beautiful? How can those stories of redemption be used as a testimony to others?

- 7 -
NEAR AND FAR

How long, O Lord? Will you forget me forever?
How long will you hide your face from me? How long must I
take counsel in my soul and have sorrow in my heart all the day?
How long shall my enemy be exalted over me? ~ Psalm 13:1-2 ESV

"Is the Lord going to use you in a great way? Quite probably. Is He going
to prepare you as you expect? Probably not." ~ Charles Swindol

When my son and daughter were little, we watched a lot of children's programming. There was *Barney*, *Dora the Explorer*, and the old classic, *Sesame Street*. During my kid's Sesame Street era, Elmo was the craze. However, I think my favorite character is still Grover. He is the bumbling, adorable, blue puppet that always did the "Near and Far" sketches.

You may or may not remember the "Near and Far" sketches. They would begin with Grover appearing super close to the camera, and in his trademark voice he would proclaim: "Near." Then he would quickly run to the furthest point in the background, turn around, cup his hands to his mouth and yell, "Far." Grover would repeat these two steps until he was panting and out of breath. I know that is a boringly simple exercise for us educated types, but I guess kids love it. Besides that, it taught children the concept of distance.

In a journey of faith, there are most definitely moments when God feels wonderfully and fearfully close. However, there are also seasons in which God appears to be distant, unhearing, and possibly even uncaring. In this chapter, I want to share how we can best navigate those quiet times— times when God's voice seems distant or absent.

Where Did God Go?

I have heard a lot of Christian anecdotal statements in my lifetime, probably more than I would ever care to admit. There is the classic, "Jesus is the reason for the season." There are also the play-on-words church-sign cliches such as "God answers knee-mail" and "CH_CH. What's Missing? UR." That just makes you want to pray or get up and head to church, doesn't it? Of course, we cannot forget the down home country saying, "If that doesn't get you fired up about God, then your wood is wet." Yes, that is actually a saying that I have heard people use at church.

I do not mean to be too cynical. I understand there is a nugget of truth in each of these statements. It is just that they are so over-the-top cheesy it is difficult for me to take them seriously. One such line that has tortured me over the years is this one: "If you feel distant from God, guess who moved?" Without a doubt, there is no subtlety in this statement. It is basically saying that if you do not feel the closeness of God, then it is your fault. The presumed circumstance is that you have wandered away from God and He is now awaiting your return.

For the record, there have been many times in my life where I went rogue and left my Father's side. There have also been times when my spiritual rebellion felt near that of the prodigal son. I will not even deny that plain old apathy has, at various times, created a wedge between God and I. However, there have been moments when the extreme relational distance I have felt with God seemed anything but my fault. There was distance, but it was not because I was not striving to close the gap.

Dealing with Distance

As I stated in earlier chapters, I grew up in church. I knew the formula for keeping God happy and on your side. You were supposed to go to Sunday School and worship service. You were to pray and read the Bible every day. General acts of kindness were a plus, as well as getting along with your family members. If you wanted to get really crazy, you could even make some huge sacrifice like miss the Super Bowl to attend Sunday evening church with the ten other people in your congregation that have never heard of football (and by *miss the Super Bowl* I mean record it and watch it later, minus all the scandalous advertising).

Yes, I knew the formula. However, there was a season in my life, about six years into full-time ministry, when the formula quit adding up. In fact, the formula did not even make sense. No matter what I tried to do to reconnect with God, nothing was working.

At the time, Michelle and I lived in the North Georgia mountains. I was the youth pastor of a county seat church. It was a good church with a mix of eager believers and denominational woes. God allowed us to have quite a season of growth and blessing within the youth ministry during our first few years there. I was about two years in and everything on the outside appeared to be going smoothly. What people did not know was that I had begun imploding on the inside.

The whole situation was exasperated by my horrible eating and lack of any healthy habits. Mix in the fact that my selfishness was in full outbreak, which caused my relationship with Michelle to suffer accordingly. Every arena of life had been shaken and stirred, leaving me swirling in the aftermath. There were days when I felt as though I was in full meltdown.

There were moments I would be preaching about the grandness of God, His forgiving nature, and His immense love for people while a spirit of confusion would descend on me. Even while declaring those words with such authority, on the inside I was doubting almost every single one of those profound truths. My soul was dryer than the desert and I had never felt more distant from God. There was not a day that went by that I did not question nearly everything I believed. I had ears alright, but I was not hearing God at all.

To make matters worse, I did not have anyone I could talk to about what was happening to me, or so I thought. See I worked in the type of church where you did not vocalize scary doubts. It was okay to wrestle with God's will and wonder whether you should be pre-millennial or not, but it was not exactly acceptable to question the very existence and nature of God, at least not openly.

There were nights when I would beg God to reveal Himself in a miraculous way. I desperately needed to hear God's voice afresh, anew. Still, the silence remained. I would moan and whine to Michelle about the state of affairs quite often. She had to get some credits toward sainthood during those months because I was most definitely miserable to live with. I felt like such the phony, but even more, so I felt empty.

Oh, and did I mention I was in seminary too? Yes, I was a youth pastor in a conservative Southern church, dying from doubt, torturing my family with my selfishness, and I was attending seminary. One day after class I even asked my professor questions about a hypothetical guy going through my exact situation, with veiled details of course. The answers I received were not much help. Actually, they were no help at all. I recall my hopeless feelings after realizing even the people training me could not really speak hope or clarity into my current situation.

During this brief yet scary season, I often entertained the idea of leaving the ministry and working at a restaurant, or anywhere. I was lost. I desperately wanted to hear from God.

Deserts Are Normal

It was not until later in ministry, probably almost four years later to be exact, that I realized my spiritual dryness had a name. Not only did it have a name, but it was normal for many people who have followed Jesus diligently for years. Some may call it a spiritual pruning. Others call it a season of testing. Yet, the best name for it, in my mind, came from St. John of the Cross. This early church father called what I was experiencing the Dark Night of the Soul. Unfortunately, this dark night did not come with a cool costume and a great car. Sadly, it came with a lot of questions.

St. John of the Cross writes about the Dark Night of the Soul as a period of spiritual desolation or crisis on one's pathway to communion with Christ. This definition best described my season of divine distance while in Georgia. It was not that I didn't want to be close to Christ. It was not as though I did not care about the condition of my soul. There just seemed to be a Sahara-sized desert of doubt suddenly between the God I loved and longed to follow and myself.

I remember sitting at The Journey, a two-year, six-retreat spiritual formation process I attended in Southern California, while men of wisdom, that I highly respected, shared about this condition. They did not simply present academic facts about the possibility of this happening to believers. No, they shared from the depths of their painful past experiences; experiences like that which haunted me in Georgia nearly four years prior.

I recall fighting back tears of relief, realizing that I was normal and that this happened to other people as well as me. There was a tremendous freedom and release during those moments. All the baggage of guilt and shame I had carried from my season of doubt was cut free by the overwhelming grace of God. It was only then that I truly realized what God was trying to do in me while in Georgia. He was trying to deepen my faith, dependence, and love for Him.

Relief in a Random Place

Deep into my dark night of the soul, I ran into the guy who served as youth pastor of the church where I worked prior to me. He and a friend had felt led of God to plant a church in a nearby town. We began talking about life, ministry, and what God was doing in and around us. The conversation slowly led to me sharing some of my current condition. For those who asked or even hinted to how I was probably got more than they bargained. It was hard to hide the festering sores of spiritual doubt that plagued me at the time.

Before the conversation was over, he had invited me to a meeting with a few other men. He explained that they met together to discuss spiritual issues just like I was having. Part of me resisted due to the ridiculous nature of possible church politics, but my soul cravings were too strong. I had to be a part of this conversation. I needed this too badly.

The first few times we met, we discussed what a true Christian is, what it meant to follow Jesus, and how that affects the modern day church experience. We actually read a book from an author whose name you had to whisper in church circles for fear of being label "a liberal," or worse "post-modern." That book stirred up the conversation and then our own reactions to it filled the time. It may have felt like an exercise in futility to some, but to me it was wonderful.

I kept attending these conversation groups. I went on a men's retreat with the guys from the plant church and I even attended Wednesday morning men's Bible study with them. The freedom I felt in those moments to both be definitive and doubtful about my faith was exactly what I needed during this season of my life. Yes, it was relief found in a random place, but I did not doubt that it was God-ordained.

My season of darkness and desert lasted for nearly a year. As quickly as the clouds of doubt seemed to settle, that was how quickly they seemed to disappear. The level of connection with Christ after that moment was even greater. It was as if a dam had broken open to release the rushing waters of God's love and wisdom again. My faith was tried and tested and I was a better man because of the trial. Although I believe I did not fully understand all that I had experienced until years later, I was grateful to feel the closeness of God again. He was no longer "far" but "near."

Words of Hope

I would venture to say that many of you reading this book right now, whether a paid church employee or lay leader, may be struggling through a season of divine distance. You may feel as though you are hearing just enough from God to pour out on those you lead, but God seems quiet in your ears. You may feel hypocritical that what you are coaching and encouraging people to do in their lives is not as present in your own. You may not feel the safety to share your doubts within the context of your current environment. Either way, I want to offer a few thoughts and a word of hope.

You are Normal

First things first, I want to assure you that you are normal. Every Christ follower, at one point or another, will face a season in which their faith will be tested and tried to prove its quality and integrity. Do not panic. Do not fret. Instead, rest in the fact that millions upon millions of believers that have gone before you have wrestled with this reality.

Everyone from St. John of the Cross to Billy Graham has felt these feelings. Even Mother Teresa, in her journals, expressed seasons of prolonged divine distance. Read a psalm or two and see if King David ever expressed concerns about the distance of God in his life. Jesus even quoted one of those Psalms

> *Every Christ follower, at one point or another, will face a season in which their faith will be tested. Rest assured; you are normal.*

from the cross when he cried out, "My God, my God, why have you forsaken me" (Psalm 22:1 NIV). Simply put, know that you are not alone.

Understand the Reason For the Season

I know the church can unintentionally be a herald for the following religious formula:

Church Attendance + Bible Study + Prayer = All Will Be Well

However, that formula is rarely the example we see the scriptures. Ask the newly anointed King David what he did to have spears thrown at him, other than follow the formula of faith. Ask Joseph, the accused rapist, how his dream and the formula of faith worked out for him. Ask the apostle Paul how the formula of Pharisaical piety played out in his life. He might enlighten you about how God had to knock him off his high horse (the puns are always intended). Paul was a man who practiced the formula but was not any closer to God.

It is important to understand that a spiritual formula does not always equal true authentic faith.

Yes, you may be experiencing divine distance from God because of your willful disobedience; sins of willful commission. Or you may be sensing a divine distance due to sins of omission.

I remember the late, great Adrian Rodgers preaching that we often do not hear a new word of direction or insight from God because we are not yet obeying His last request. I would be remiss not to acknowledge that sometimes the gap in our relationship with God can actually be our doing.

However, many within a Dark Night of the Soul are experiencing what I have found to be the real life lesson. Most of the time, the divine distance is created by God to see if we will pursue Him alone.

Will He be our only source of joy and fulfillment?

Will we find our sole significance, purpose, identity, and hope in the person of Christ?

81

Will the good news that Christ is enough
for us truly ring out in our hearts?

Will the distance we feel make us explorers
of the divine mystery that is God?

Or will we settle for a land more comfortable, more formulaic?

David Wilcox, a brilliant singer, song-writer, describes the theme of the Dark Night perfectly in one of his songs. He writes:

Prosperity will have its seasons
Even when it's here, it's going by
When it's gone, we pretend we know the reasons
And all the roots grow deeper when it's dry, when it's dry.

All the roots grow deeper when it is dry. That is a profound way to illustrate what happens in the heart during a season of divine distance. Tour a vineyard and the owner will tell you that there are moments during the life of a grape when farmers will deprive the fruit of water. It can sound counter-productive, but the deprivation is purposeful. It forces the roots of the vine to grow deep in search of water in order to then produce a quality sugar within each and every grape.

The divine deprivation initiated by our Father, the gardener, cannot be viewed in the negative. We must come to see that it is for our betterment. Deeper roots assist our survival, but they also guarantee that the fruit of our life will be sweeter. I think this is what Jesus meant when He looked at the disciples on the night before His death told them that He appointed them to produce fruit, fruit that will last. However, that type of abundant living and eternal fruitfulness takes deep roots.

Express Yourself

Often times when wrestling through a Dark Night of the Soul, you may feel like you have no one with whom to talk. That could not be farther from the truth. There are thousands of Christian counselors, pastors, and spiritual directors that understand the season you are in and would love to help. Yes, you may need to step outside of your current ministry context or regular circle of friends to find these people, but they are there. Do not be afraid to find a safe place to talk it out. Vocalizing your struggle not only helps you process through it, the exposure causes the struggle to lose its power over you. Yes, you have ears to listen, but in this case, use your mouth as well.

God Is With Us

As much as I have written about the perceived distance we experience during the dry times, it is important to underscore that God *is* truly with you. He never takes a day off or leaves on vacation. No matter the circumstance, the sin, or the desperateness of your situation, know that God will never leave nor forsake you. In the book "When the Well Runs Dry," Thomas Green writes concerning St. John of Cross' "The Dark Night of the Soul" saying:

"John's explanation implies that the darkness is not really darkness, that God is not really absent, but that we lack the eyes to see, the tongue to taste what is really there. That is precisely the point. God is not absent; he is closer than he has ever been, but we are blind."

Even when you may not exactly see or hear Him, Jesus is still *Emmanuel*, God with us.

Maybe the Sesame Street sketches I alluded to earlier were not just for my kids. Maybe Grover running near and far was a lesson for me to glean as well. Remember, seasons of divine distance are normal– all the roots grow deeper when it is dry. Finally, do not be afraid to talk out your doubts with those who have seen both the dark night and the rising sun.

QUESTIONS TO PONDER

Have you ever experienced a Dark Night of the Soul? How did it disrupt your daily routines, faith, relationships with others? How did you resolve it? Has it been resolved yet?

Do you feel you have people in your life that you could talk with if you had doubts or questions about your faith?

How has God challenged you to dig deep roots? What, if any, sweeter fruit have you seen after a season of deepened roots?

What are some scripture passages God has used to comfort you during seasons of divine distance to keep you pursuing His divine mystery?

For more about the dry times of the soul, read "When The Well Runs Dry" by Thomas H. Green, S.J.

Part Two

Communally

- 8 -
THE CHEESE STANDS ALONE

*So then you are no longer strangers and aliens, but you are fellow
citizens with the saints and members of the household of God.
~ Ephesians 2:19 ESV*

*"Let him who cannot be alone beware of community... Let him who is
not in community beware of being alone... Each by itself has
profound perils and pitfalls. One who wants fellowship without
solitude plunges into the void of words and feelings, and the one who
seeks solitude without fellowship perishes in the abyss of vanity, self-
infatuation and despair." ~ Dietrich Bonhoeffer*

I was flipping through channels one Saturday and for a split
second landed on PBS. Now PBS is not my normal viewing
choice. I do not have anything against public television, it is just that
I was switching between two football games and some children's
programming got in the way. I do not mean that rudely. I just mean
that I was not able to turn the channel fast enough and for a
moment heard someone singing "The Farmer in the Dell."

It was only three to four seconds of the song tops; however, it
was stuck in my head for hours. I found myself humming it;
muttering the lyrics I remembered and ad-libbing the ones I did
not. I became so obsessed with this silly song that day that I actually
googled the full lyrics. It starts off with a farmer in the dell, his
home. Then this farmer takes for himself a wife. The wife takes a
child, and the child takes a cow. Why the child chooses a cow, I
could not tell you, but it happens. The song continues on with each
of the animals mentioned choosing a partner; a pig, dog, cat, and a
mouse. Finally, the song ends with the mouse choosing cheese and
the cheese standing alone. That is the lyrical wonder which makes
up "The Farmer in the Dell."

I can see why the mouse picked cheese. I mean who doesn't like
cheese, unless you are a vegan, of course. However, why does the
cheese have to stand alone? Maybe because it is about to get eaten

by the mouse. The phrase about the cheese standing alone really stuck with me that day, like a barbwire fence some may say. Maybe it sounds a bit better to refer to it the way folk artist David Wilcox does: "I was bugged for a metaphorical reason."

Now do not get the wrong idea. I am not feeling for the cheese because of its possible stench or potential doom. The truth is I did not want the cheese to stand alone, but mostly because I do not want to be alone. At our core, I believe we are all that way. No one likes being alone. Now there are times when closing the door to the world and hiding out for a few hours of quiet or napping is amazing, but I am talking about a condition of the soul rather than moments of recovery. I enjoy time alone, I just do not like being alone.

Only the Lonely

It is truly amazing, in a world filled with countless ways to stay connected, that we could even feel alone. This is an age flooded with connection points. Social media gives us access to the entire globe at the click of a button or in 140 character bursts. We can let people know about who we are, what we like, and what we are doing—even when it is pointless. We can communicate with old friends from high school, family across the country, and business partners nations away. With all this social connectivity, how could anyone be alone?

Do not forget the plethora of social entertainment options afforded to us today. For a minimal investment, you can venture out of the home into crowds of people in theaters, shopping centers, music venues, and sporting events. It does not take much to be surrounded by thousands of people; just head to the mall on Black Friday. Yet I would submit that even when surrounded by a throng of humanity, if surveyed, many people would say they still feel alone.

There is also the reinvention of the third places in our society. It used to be that the bar was that place to go after work to hang out with friends. With the rise of destination restaurants, niche exercise chains, and the ever popular coffeehouse, the third place market has grown. Now I love a trip to Starbucks and a chat with my barista as much as the next person. In fact, much of the narrative of this book was written in such a place. However, I never felt a true sense of community in the coffee shop while typing my meager manifesto. In many ways, despite being in my third place mini-crowd, I was still alone.

The phrase destination restaurant might have caught your attention. Every town or city has them. I call them destination spots because these businesses target a special demographic of people they hope will make their eatery the post-work stop or weekend hub. Whether it's embracing the end of work week, cheering on a favorite sports team, or the center of what is trendy, these places draw a crowd. Yet, I would argue that quite a few patrons still feel, even battle, loneliness there.

If you do not believe me, try this simple two-fold test. The next time you visit a destination restaurant, coffeehouse, or another third place, take a look around. First of all, who is on their phone? Despite being in the middle of a room full of people and potential relationships, many will still escape to the safety of people not in the room. They click away on touch-screen technology, chatting with others about moments past or plotting those yet to come. It is rare to see people genuinely embracing the present with those around them.

The second half of the test is to count the number of people engaged in actual conversation. Now I am not referring to conversations about how much they love or hate the team that is currently winning. Nor do I mean those moaning about work or musing about the weather. Instead, who is really talking? Who is sharing about their family? Who is unpacking their dreams and hopes for life? Which group is sharing about victories or struggles? Who is demonstrating great vulnerability and trust? I would argue that until those conversations are happening, then people will continually feel alone no matter how cool the crowd, no matter how happening the place.

Though chosen, the cheese stands alone. We, too, as the saints of God, though chosen, often stand alone. I Peter 2:9 states, "We are a chosen people... a people belonging to God" (NIV). It is a marvelous truth to truly understand that we are a chosen people. Despite being chosen, we too easily identify with the mouse's lonely cheese. The nagging feeling of being alone stealthily creeps into our hearts and tries to camp out. It is in the lonely camp that we lose sight of our Father and forget that we truly are the adopted sons and daughters of God. It is here that we end up not listening for

God's voice, only to settle for the seductive whispers of lesser gods. Before long, our lonely condition manifests itself in strange ways, especially within the church. By strange, I mean highly self-focused.

The Church as "We", Not "It" or "I"

I have worked on enough church staffs and been in one too many staff meetings to know that the American institution of church cares much about the individualistic desires of its attendees. It can argue for deeper values of mission and compassion, but all too often the attractional Western church settles for the far less noble practiced values; values that exalt self, self-centeredness, and satisfaction of personal not corporate needs.

Therefore, conversations about Sally Saint's preference for music or Bobby Believer's desire for deeper teaching become centerpiece whether we admit it or not. In time, and with enough complaining, adaptations are made to meet the needs or wants of the vocal few. I would argue that these subtle changes in ministry, though not inherently bad, reinforce a system of "alone-ness" versus "chosen-ness", one about personal consumption over communal mission.

Be careful how you hear these next statements. They come from a strong sense of care for people and not an agenda protection place. For just a moment, open yourself to seeing this common church situation differently.

Let us say that Bobby Believer wants deeper teaching. Bobby whines to multiple staff members about the days when there was deeper teaching at church. His complaint is obviously a symptom of a greater personal need. Maybe his need revolves around growing older or even feeling like his church no longer considers or cares for him with its programming choices. It could also be that no one has ever challenged Bobby to be a mentor to younger men as people were to him at one point. So instead of a spring of wisdom, Bobby has become a reservoir of stagnant knowledge.

No matter what the issue truly is, because the church is often better at medicating the symptoms of its problems than tackling the sickness, it will bend towards Bobby with some sort of veiled compromise. Bobby will feel validated, and everyone moves on until Bobby has another issue.

What happens if the church chooses not to bend? Well, then Bobby feels unwelcome, unimportant, and alone. Bobby's feeling of aloneness will push him to do one of two things. He will find a new place of worship; one that will listen to him. We would all agree that this type of separation is never the goal. Rather, we would like to see Bobby come to trust that the leadership he has submitted to is asking him to see the greater needs of the community around him in their programming designs. In other words, Bobby is not alone. He is a part of something larger than just himself. He is a member of the body of Christ.

If a church leadership team agrees that Bobby is right and deeper teaching is needed, all is good. However, if a leadership team disagrees with Bobby and adapts to him anyway, they are now meeting the need of the one versus the many. It is important to remember that the church, God's people, is not about the one, but the many. He chose us all.

That is not something we are great at in the American church. We have forgotten that church is not something you attend, but a group of believers set apart by God to become Christ-like "together."

People often say, "We just do not want anyone to feel alone at church." The truth is, I have said it. It is at those moments that I have to stop and remind myself that the church is the whole of all the saints

The Church must learn to surrender her desires for the greater good

past, present, and future, resurrected to new life because of the mighty work of Jesus on the cross and over the grave. We have been awakened to live as citizens of the colony of heaven despite our current refugee status in this world. Centuries of saints, both living and long dead, make up the church eternal. Church is not, and can never be, an "it." Church is always a "we." We can never do church alone. Church can only happen when we realize we have been chosen by God to live in communion together as His children—pushing toward ultimate Christ-like maturity.

Individuals: Right?

We live in a nation of individualism that celebrates our "rights" to do many things; gather, speak, worship, protest, own guns. While none of these are bad qualities entirely as it pertains to a democratic society, this mentality can be harmful in the church. In the church, we must approach the scripture through the lens of community versus that of individual rights. When we do, very familiar stories and verses from the Bible take on much deeper meaning.

I began to notice this all the more as I learned to listen to the Lord's voice more clearly. Take for instance the story of the Exodus. In all my days of church, it felt like Moses was touted as the hero of the story for standing up to Pharaoh and leading the Israelites out of Egypt and into the Promised Land. Sermon after sermon was given about how we are to be like Moses in the midst of adversity, in the face of our own personal Pharaohs. Children's songs were sung about Moses telling Pharaoh to let the people go. However, I would argue this is a product of individualistic and "aloneness" thinking, not communal thinking.

The real hero in the story, well every scripture story, is our great God. The victory is not that a royal-raised, unconvicted murderer with a speech impediment rallied a throng of slaves to freedom. If that were the case, then we would have to quickly overlook the story of Moses being banished from a future inheritance of the Promised Land because of his selfish act of individualism at the Meribah rock (Numbers 20:1-13). That story is not recorded to elevate the character of Moses, but to demonstrate that a moment of individualism had high costs. The Exodus story is much bigger and broader than Moses alone. It is about God choosing a people, and the people's hero, Yahweh.

The true victory in the Exodus account is that God toppled the idols of Egypt, rescued His people, the Israelites, and brought them out of bondage that they might worship Him together as a peculiar people, different from all the peoples of the world. That is a theme that is found later in scripture as well. In the gospels, Jesus toppled the current idols of Pharisaical religion and Roman rule, and rescued mankind by His substitutionary death and ultimate resurrection. Jesus' sacrifice was definitely a selfless act. He was alone upon the cross so we would never have to be alone.

Christ's victorious rising led to the birth of the church, His called out ones, gathering to exalt Him forever. I feel we have made so much about Jesus as our own personal Savior that we have forgotten God has saved us to join His family, not start our own. It is sad to watch "individual-focused" churches adopt this mentality. Instead of looking to advance the Kingdom of Heaven, they seek to grow their own kingdom. Instead of learning to be the people of God on a mission together, They become a group of individuals seeking to bolster the name and programs of their church.

Another way we see the rise of individualism in American religion is in the interpretation of scripture. Many of the popular verses we snatch from the Old Testament and try to make into personal life verses were messages delivered by prophets to nations and people groups. For example, Jeremiah 29:11 reads, "I know the plans I have for you declares the Lord. Plans to prosper you, not to harm you. Plans for a hope and a future." The "you" in those verses is best read "you all." So are virtually all of the "you" Greek words in Paul's epistles that make up the majority of the New Testament as well. Those words were delivered to the many, not a single person. Verses like that are not meant for a single person alone. They should and must always be read with a "we the people focus." Self-focused biblical interpretations will eventually end in greater "alone-ness", not "chosen-ness."

Listening must always include the whole community of saints

When it comes to listening to the Lord, it too can never remain on the personal level only. Listening must always advance to include the whole community of saints. I would submit that some of my greatest discoveries in Scripture have come through moments of listening to the Lord with other believers. God has done so much to demonstrate His nature and character to me as I watch and listen to Him reveal Himself to others.

I will explain this more in the next chapter. For now, I hope you see that we cannot stand alone. We were not made to be just elevated individuals. We were designed for our diversity to excel in the midst of community. We are not "The Cheese." We cannot stand alone.

QUESTIONS TO PONDER

Do you wrestle with feelings of loneliness? Have you ever? Have you ever intentionally, or unintentionally been "the cheese"?

How has social media communication hindered your ability to converse with others on a deeper, more personal level about real life issues?

How do you feel about the idea of "alone-ness" and "chosen-ness" as discussed in this chapter?

How have you maybe inadvertently contributed to the idea of individual rights over the rights of the community in your church?

How can the church best remind herself that every member is needed and crucial?

- 9 -
LISTENING TO GOD THROUGH OTHERS

Therefore, having put away falsehood,
let each one of you speak the truth with his neighbor,
for we are members one of another. ~ Ephesians 4:25 ESV

"Be in the heart of each to whom I speak;
In the mouth of each who speaks unto me.
This day be within and without me,
lowly and meek, yet all powerful."
~ Canticle of St. Patrick

During my senior year of high school, I made a few extra bucks working as a tutor for a fifth grader. That was way more of a challenge than I had expected. We would meet at the public library and I would help him process math, navigate geography, and make sense of all his English homework. In many ways, I felt more like an interpreter than a tutor. It was as if I was rephrasing what his teachers and textbooks had said in a way he could understand.

If we are honest, we have all needed that kind of help along the way. I could help a grade-school student with his math, but I needed a friend to break down the joys of high school trigonometry to me. I can surf the web, but do not ask me to program the actual code of a website. I know I need to file taxes every year, but do not expect me to fully understand the tax code. For those tasks, I would need a tutor.

Do you remember the first time you bought a car or even a home? The amount of paperwork you signed during those moments is ridiculous. I remember being given a legal-size sheet of paper filled with words. Our lawyer stated that my signature at the bottom of the page was simply me agreeing to pay the house payment. What a novel idea. Why couldn't that be the only sentence on the page: "If you agree to pay the monthly house payment, then check *yes* and *sign*." That whole moment would have been thoroughly overwhelming without an interpreter, someone who could speak truth through the jumble.

Speaking of interpreters, my favorite moment with an interpreter happened during a mission trip to South Africa. A pastor friend and I had traveled to Venda, the Northern agricultural region of the country. This specific area of South Africa was more primitive than where a majority of our work was done in Johannesburg and Pretoria. Our task was to lead a group of pastors in a seminar through the book of Romans.

Our translator was the pastor of a prominent local congregation. His name was Joseph. Now Joseph was a fiery man, full of the Spirit. He preached like a stereotypical American pastor from the South, time warped back from the 1980s. He would raise his voice to drive home the point, pace back and forth, and for good measure, he would occasionally lean in and point aggressively at the congregation. Do not get me wrong, Joseph was a passionate man of God. It is just that his interpretive skills were unique.

My desire, when it comes to preaching, is to deliver truth clearly and simply so that all people may be inspired to respond to Jesus and His gospel. With that said, I am a somewhat low-key speaker; rarely raising my voice or pacing the stage. That does not mean I lack conviction or passion, I am just a more temperate teacher. But with Joseph as my interpreter, low-key was not enough.

Whenever I, in my style, would share a statement of truth that Joseph liked, he would first say amen and then declare the translation so loud into his microphone that I would almost wince. If he felt I was too brief, he would expand the idea for me. I once shared the phrase, "This is true because our God loves us deeply." That one sentence in English turned into a lengthy translated paragraph in his native tongue.

I remember watching him wondering when he would stop and what exactly he was saying to these pastors and church leaders. After a moment, Joseph caught me looking at him. When he finished speaking, he turned and loudly whispered to me that had taken a moment to share just *how* deeply God loved us and how much we had been forgiven. I chuckled on the inside and continued. Teaching with Joseph was a great experience.

Translators can be needed in our adventure of learning to listen to the Lord as well. We often need someone to translate truth for us; restating the obvious or even the complex so we truly get it. A traditional method that has been adopted in most Christian circles today is for a pastor or a gifted teacher to break down the principles of the Bible into bite-size chunks of wisdom. Where this method is both great and biblical, we have also seen it is kryptonite as well.

Congregations that are hyper-focused on a pastor can create an unhealthy dependence on one leader to be the key truth-teller. As much as I heard negative statements growing up in Baptist circles about priests acting as modern day mediators between God and man, I could not help but see the hypocrisy of pastors willing to be the spoon-feeder of truth for their congregation. *What was the difference?* I would wonder.

This dangerous dependence happens in the conference and seminar circuit as well. As much as it is fun to see what the newest author or popular keynote speaker has to say, there is something to be said for the voice of the Lord spoken to us by lay men and women. That is one of the benefits of practicing *Sticks, Stars, and Signs* in community.

In the Mouth of Those Who Speak Unto Me

As part of the *Lectio Divina* process shared earlier, the liturgy included a canticle from St. Patrick (see appendix). This canticle, or hymn, reading was always used to conclude our corporate time together. One specific phrase from the hymn reads: (Christ) "Be in the heart of each to whom I speak; in the mouth of each who speaks unto me." The first time I heard it I was caught off guard because I found it both profound and shocking.

First of all, I realized I was basically asking God to prepare the hearts of people I speak with to hear God's Word spoken from me. Once I honestly meditated on the request I was making of the Lord, the true weight of it sunk in. My words to those with whom I have relationship, as well as the unsuspecting, were to be shared as if they were messages from God. That is why Paul challenges the church of Ephesus to "let no corrupting talk come out of your mouths, but only such as is good for building up, as fits the occasion, that it may give grace to those who hear" (Ephesians 4:29 ESV). It is also why Peter encourages the early church to "always being prepared to make a defense to anyone who asks you for a reason for the hope that is in you; yet do it with gentleness and respect" (1 Peter 3:15 ESV).

The second line from the canticle that shocked me had to do with the fact I was asking God to speak to me through the mouth of others. That is not a common request we make when we pray. How often do you enter into conversation with another hoping or even expecting God to use their words to challenge or comfort you, outside of a sermon or Bible study? It was not, and sadly still is not, my standard mode of operation. However, living in community as the church has made me more expectant of a word from God from the lips of others.

Lectio Divina Groups

One way that I began to foster this idea of expectancy in the college and young adult ministry I led in California was to start my own *Lectio Divina* group with my leadership team. Before long, is was more than natural for us to be sharing life and truth together. It is not enough to share life and just spend time, meals, and moments together. We must also be willing to share with others the truth God has spoken to us.

Jon Byron also had a spiritual mentor growing up. His name is Chuck Miller. Chuck calls this exchange of truth among the saints "sharing bread." I have heard Chuck ask many times, "What is the bread that God is baking in the oven of your life?" It makes sense. If God is our provider of daily bread, both physically and spiritually, shouldn't we have something to say when people ask, "What scripture are you meditating on right now?"

The college and young adult ministry *Lectio Divina* group spent powerful times in the Word of God as well as life-changing times in community. I was always amazed at what words or phrases that would be drawn out during the first reading of a passage (Sticks). Without fail, someone would share a phrase from the text that I had not even seen. It was like we were all watching the same movie, but from different camera angles.

Without the various perspectives of my brothers and sisters in the room, I maybe would have glossed over a portion of the passage that my heart or mind did not want to address. At other times, the repetition of everyone saying the same word or phrase aloud made me realize the weight and significance of the text we were reading together. There were times when I would write down verbatim what someone else in the group was sharing from God; it would be that profound and powerful. God was speaking to me from the mouth of a friend.

When it came time for the emotional listening segment of the *Lectio Divina* practice (Stars), I was almost always stunned at how vulnerable and open people were. As a part of their emotional discovery of the text, people would confess deep struggles, share humbling truths, or reveal God-given dreams for their lives. I never ceased to be amazed at the level of transparency the Holy Spirit generated during our Lectio gatherings.

Invitations to obedience delivered from God, and then shared in community, are sobering and powerful (Signs). It is truly amazing how God accomplishes His work of maturity in all of us at different places and paces. Usually, where God was inviting me to raise the bar was where another person had shared they were experiencing victory. The added bonus of their testimony increased my resolve to obey my own invitation. Without fail, I was always convicted and inspired by the invitations of God to my friends at the table.

One other interesting phenomenon took place during Lectio group times. The sharing of emotional insights and personal invitations from the Lord in a group setting almost always served as a prayer request time without anyone having to ask, "Who has any prayer requests?" Every time someone shared openly from the heart, I knew specifically how to pray for them. The genuine vulnerability of those moments even stirred a new found desire to be an intercessor for fellow brothers or sisters in Christ. Many a spontaneous prayer meeting was had after a tearful sharing time during our Lectio Divina gatherings.

Sharing life in a Christ-centered community became a one powerful way to hear God speak.

More than anything, these groups fostered such a real, strong bond of community among all who participated that it was nearly tangible. I can still picture the faces of those young adults and feel deep affection for them. Some of my favorite moments with the children of God have been in these living and active Lectio groups. I can only imagine what my experience with God's people in heaven will be

101

like after having experienced the richness of community with His saints here.

Learning from Life Stories

Yet another way in which God continues speaks to me is through the life stories and experiences of others. You cannot watch the Olympics, whether summer or winter, without hearing about the painful backstories of many of the participating athletes. Their stories include everything from cancer battles to government oppression, family tragedy to overcoming tragic injury. We would all say that there is something motivating about seeing someone persevere through real pain. There is always a lesson to be learned. C.S. Lewis is famous for saying that, "God whispers to us in our pleasures, speaks in our conscience, but shouts in our pains: it is his megaphone to rouse a deaf world."

When I see a couple's marriage on the rocks and they press through the storm safely to the other side, I rejoice and resolve to love my wife even more. When I see a Senior Saint go to be with the Lord after years of faithful service to the Kingdom, I commit to keep running the race with greater endurance. Whenever the tales of Christian martyrdom anywhere in the world fall on my ears, I am all the more determined to live for the glory of my King. When I witness the destructive nature of cancer attack the body but not the spirit of a believer, I pray that I would cling to Jesus that tightly during my personal trials.

There is little to nothing more compelling than the stories of people to highlight the truth that God is trying to speak into my life. Their stories make me want to live a better story. Their stories are powerful because they are connected to the Author of Life who is telling the greatest redemptive story ever. I suppose that is why we call His story the gospel, the good news.

It is through these various means of relationship that God allows His voice to fall on my ears. Because of my devotion to community with others, I now have even better ears to hear Him speak, especially through mouths and lives of others.

QUESTIONS TO PONDER

Are you part of a group of people that share truth together on a regular basis?

What does that or could that look like for you right now?

Share a time when God used someone to deliver a timely/powerful word of truth to you.

Has anyone ever thanked you for being a mouthpiece for God to them?

How does this idea of being a mouthpiece for God's message change the intentionality and practices of your speech?

How has the life story of another believer compelled you toward greater intimacy with God?

- 10 -
CAN YOU SEE IT NOW?

*So Philip ran to him and heard him reading Isaiah the prophet
and asked, "Do you understand what you are reading?"
And he said, "How can I, unless someone guides me?" And he invited
Philip to come up and sit with him. ~ Acts 8:30-31 ESV*

*"We need someone who encourages us when we are tempted
to give it all up, to forget it all, to just walk away in despair.
We need someone who discourages us when we move too rashly
in unclear directions or hurry proudly to a nebulous goal.
We need someone who can suggest to us when to read
and when to be silent, which words to reflect upon and
what to do when silence creates much fear and little peace."
~ Henri Nouwen*

Don't you just love that moment when you lose your keys? You spend your morning rushing around the house getting ready to leave, and then realize your keys are nowhere to be found. If you happen to be anything like me, you move into mini panic-attack mode. The search, both high and low, commences. You retrace your steps, blame everyone else in the house for moving them, and feel silly when someone helping you points out they are in your pocket.

It is strange how we need others to point out the obvious in our lives at times. It should be obvious that our sunglasses are on top of our head as we rummage around looking for them. It ought to be obvious that if you eat red onions and garlic for lunch no one will want to be around you at work. It should also be obvious speeding that by a policeman will get you a ticket. In the same way, it ought to be

We often need another's perspective to aid in our personal discovery of the authentic work of God in us.

obvious when God is doing a work in our lives; getting our attention, speaking needed truth, or rebuking our rebellion. However, many times this is not the case.

We need someone who can stand on the outside of our lives and point to the obvious for us. In my journey, spiritual direction has been the tool God has used for this very purpose. Let me explain a bit more.

Spiritual What? Oh, Direction

The first time I heard the phrase spiritual direction was in 2007. It was in the context of a two-year spiritual formation process hosted by The Leadership Institute in Southern California. Jon, my Yoda-mentor, was a founding member of the organization, and I was encouraged to attend the program.

Now I was familiar with the idea that God is the one who gives us direction, purpose, and mission in life. However, this was something different entirely. Spiritual direction is the process of accompanying people on their spiritual journey. This practice exists in the context of a spiritual friendship and emphasizes helping one discover a deeper, more intimate relationship with Christ. Jon defines spiritual direction as "time with a director who comes alongside and listens with the directed, encouraging them to attend to the Holy Spirit's process of soul transformation."

As part of the course work for this two-year Journey process, I had to read David Benner's book on the subject of Spiritual Direction entitled "Sacred Companions." It is an excellent work. He defines classic spiritual direction as:

"… an ancient form of Christian soul care that goes back to the earliest days of the church. (It) is a one-on-one relationship organized around prayer and conversation directed toward deepening intimacy with God. Spiritual directors… do not follow a standardized curriculum or implement a prepackaged program…. And most important, they seek to help those with whom they journey to discern the presence and leading of the Spirit of God— the One Jesus sent as our true spiritual director. (David Benner, Sacred Companions, pg. 17)

It is important to understand that this time-honored practice is not a form of therapy, counseling, mentoring, or advice-giving.

While all of those methodologies can be healthy and even spiritual in nature, the role of the director is not to outline a behavioral modification pattern for a person. It is not the role of the director to diagnose someone with the condition of "spiritual apathy" or "God-As-Your-Heavenly-Father" issues.

Instead, spiritual direction becomes the art of helping people notice the work of God in their lives. I like to describe it as more of an art than a hard science for two reasons. First of all, the approach with each person is different; unique to their personality and needs. No one person is the same and it requires a special flexibility and keen sensitivity to know how to help each individual, within the context of relationship.

The second reason I feel that spiritual direction is an art is I believe the Holy Spirit is the one who gives birth to the imaginative and the artistic. He is also the one who awakens the spiritual desires within those created in His image. Therefore, the more the director trusts in the leading of Holy Spirit, the more he or she will be able to sense and see what that same Spirit is doing in the life of another. Then, and only then, can they shine a light on the presence of God's deep work of redemption in the directed.

I have personally experienced the artistic work of spiritual direction in my life, both as the directed and the director. The direction moments almost always came out of intentional conversations with men or women, of which I had spiritual friendships. It was during these times that I felt the depth of brotherhood and sisterhood for the body of Christ in a very real way. The way God powerfully revealed Himself in the midst of those friendships was truly amazing.

As the directed, there were times when the Father would reassure me of His deep love, confidence, and care for me. At other points Jesus would hold up a mirror to my soul, revealing a man of character far different than Himself. Yet all the while I never felt pushed or prodded by man. I never felt as though I were being given a "spiritual to-do list" or a "find-peace-fast" formula. Instead, I was graciously invited into greater intimacy and obedience by God Himself.

As the director, a whole different dynamic took place. I found myself in deep compassion and prayer for a friend, a friend created in the very image of God. My active-listening skills were put to the test. I was not just listening to the story of someone's life, I was listening for the cues of the Holy Spirit. What would God have me to say to this person that he or she could truly know the depth of love He has for them? How could I help my friend hear Jesus' wisdom and not my moral musings or bright ideas?

One part of you may be thinking, *This is what I do with my friends when we get coffee.* I would agree that you may have spiritual conversations and you may be friends. However, I would say that there is a strong difference between chatting and spiritual direction. The gifted way in which a director highlights God's work in another's life takes training and practice. There are even schools dedicated to this fine art.

The other part of you might be thinking, *This spiritual direction thing sounds somewhat strange.* It did to me at first, too. It did not help that I googled the term. I found all kinds of information about its roots, which were

The conversation was the canvas and the work of the Holy Spirit in our midst became the colorful artwork in us both.

apparently horrid to the staunch conservative blogger or two I read. However, after digging a bit deeper, I also found information on people who provided direction, places to be trained as a director, and testimonies of many blessed by the practice. Additionally, there were countless articles about the history of spiritual direction and it's development in the church. Yet it was not until I experienced it personally a few times that the simplicity and impact of this sacred art came to life.

Jon, who serves as my director still today, would guide our time together in his office at church. It was completely non-threatening. Why should it be threatening anyway? It is a conversation with a respected friend. He would often ask what passages of scripture have been stirring me lately. Sometimes he would begin by asking what big events were happening in my life. As basic or pedestrian as those topics may sound, the chatting always reached a place of personal depth. The specificity and timeliness of each discussion always reassured me that we serve an all-knowing God, and Jon knew Him.

Spiritual Direction in the Scriptures

The more I experienced the joy of direction, the more that I noticed examples of this spiritual practice in the scriptures. One such example was shared with me by Jon during my two-year Journey process. It is the story of the walk to Emmaus recorded in the final chapter of the book of Luke.

Here two men are walking from Jerusalem, chatting about the recent crucifixion of Jesus. Then a stranger begins to walk with them, but to their surprise he has not heard of the crucifixion or any of the religious commotion which has recently taken place in Jerusalem. Luke lets us know that this stranger is Jesus, and He has hidden His identity from these men.

In accordance with the art of spiritual direction, Jesus asks the men what is on their minds and what is troubling them. They share of all the recent affairs in Jerusalem and how they thought Jesus might have been the Messiah. Jesus lets them start the conversation, and then He points out the obvious to them. In Luke 24:25-26 (ESV) Jesus even says, "O foolish ones, and slow of heart to believe all that the prophets have spoken! Was it not necessary that the Christ should suffer these things and enter into his glory?"

Then Luke writes that Jesus explained the teachings of the Scriptures to them before revealing that He was in fact the risen Christ, finishing off His time with them by disappearing from sight. I love when the men realize they have been with Jesus the whole time and one of them states: "Did not our hearts burn within us while talked to us on the road, while opened to us the Scriptures?" (Luke 24:32, ESV)

This is spiritual direction. Jesus meets men in the chaos of where they were in life, points them to Himself, and then reveals His glory to them in such a way that greater intimacy with Christ is now their one desire.

Another example of spiritual direction is found in yet another work of Luke. In Acts 8, an Ethiopian Eunuch has just spent a few days on a pilgrimage to the city of Jerusalem. There he has obtained a copy of the scroll of Isaiah. In chapter eight we find him on a desert road making his way back home to Ethiopia, attempting to make sense of the writings of Isaiah.

In the meantime, God has stationed a man of passion and power, named Philip, onto that road near the Ethiopian. Now Philip had been leading a successful revival service where many pagan sorcerers were getting saved and a city was revolutionized by the gospel of Jesus Christ. For whatever reason, God saw fit to remove Philip from the revival to place him on the road to meet with the Eunuch.

Philip hears the man reading from the scroll and asks him if he understands it. Naturally, the Eunuch's response is no. He did not know the message of the Messiah. Luke then writes that Philip proceeded to get into the Eunuch's chariot and explain to him all the teachings of the law and prophets about Jesus Christ. Before long, the chariot comes to a halt, the Eunuch is baptized, and Philip is transported to yet another place of mission.

In this story, Philip allows the Eunuch to ask questions to which Philip then points the man to Jesus, as illustrated by the Law and Prophets. Before the encounter is said and done, one more person has experienced greater intimacy with Jesus. That is spiritual direction at its finest.

From Directed to Director

A great joy came when I began to realize that my conversational moments with the people I pastored began to look a lot like spiritual direction. Now my journey from directed to director did not take on an academic component at first. I started by spending time in direction myself. I received instruction and education on the practice during my participation in The Leadership Institute's Journey process. However, I would say the greatest training I received was from the Lord Himself.

Jesus had allowed Jon and others to help me notice His deep work in my life. Now it was time for me to help others see God's work in their lives. He had placed me in a position as pastor to college students and young adults. Without fail, at least one person in this age and stage of life was always caught at a crossroads. If it was not career decisions, it was relationship matters. If it was not relationship matters, then it was identity issues. If it was not identity issues, then it was struggles with addictive behaviors or emotional baggage. The worst case scenario was a combo of all arenas of decision. There seemed to be no

My heart was that they would always listen and respond to God's wooing. I only wanted to help people notice the voice of the Good Shepherd.

greater demographic in our church in need of spiritual guidance.

I began to address people's questions about marriage, work, the Christian life, and personal struggles from a spiritual direction standpoint. It was my goal to help them hear God's Word for them at that moment. I never wanted anyone to walk away from our conversation thinking, "Wow, Shawn gives great advice" or "I'm going to do what Shawn said."

The more I prayed and practiced this way, the more I noticed a familiar pattern revealed. As these students would share I would listen closely. Before long, something they said would stick out. Maybe it would be a comment that uncovered a false belief about God. Maybe they would admit to hidden emotional hurts, hurts that had led to their current unwanted condition. Often what would be revealed was evidence this particular person did not fully believe God loved them unconditionally. No matter what was shared, before long something always stuck out.

After noticing these *"Stick"* places in our conversations, I would simply reflect the statement back to the person with whom I was sitting. I would say something like, "I heard you say that you often question whether God cares about you and your problems. Am I hearing you right?" Or maybe I would ask a question like this: "You mentioned all the good things you do for God. While that is wonderful, what if you did not do anything for God for a month? Would He still love you the same?"

Any statement I would make was always designed to help the directed person take notice where I thought God was trying to speak to them. Without fail, the person would process through my reflection of their own statement until they landed on a truth from God. More often than not a short period of silence would occur as they digested the word of truth, from God, not me. It was then that I would ask, "How does that (truth) make you feel? What emotions are rising to the surface as you think about this topic?"

Do you see the pattern yet? Sticks. Stars. Signs.

It goes without saying that we are emotional creatures. We have strong opinions. We feel deeply about our personal life crossroads, and we will either express or repress those feelings. Now some people release their emotions like a geyser and others are as stiff as a granite mountain. No matter what the expression, we must process our feelings appropriately. Helping people to do that in front of you and God helps them realize this is a conversation they can have with the Lord when you are not in the room, which is yet another benefit of spiritual direction.

One of the most important observations I have made as it pertains to the emotional piece of spiritual direction is to allow people the freedom to experience them. Whether it be crying over relationship problems or venting extreme amounts of hurt and anger, giving people the permission to show their emotions without judgment brought a powerful freedom to the moment. To be honest, I think some of the deepest work I witnessed God do, happened right in the middle of their emotional overflow. It was if I was watching a Psalmist move from anguish to exuberance in a matter of minutes.

When it comes to the "*Signs*" aspect of spiritual direction, my question was usually, "What do you feel that God would have you to do right now? What are you sensing as the next step He would have you to take?" Without fail, God would lead the person I was directing to a place of invitation that demanded both surrender and obedience.

In the rare moments that someone would struggle to see the next step God had for them, I would offer a challenge or a suggestion. My mentors, Chuck Miller and Jon Byron, have both encouraged me to frame any invitational advice in spiritual direction within the language of an experiment. So I would say something like, "Maybe this week you could experiment with praying peace over your boss at work and see how that might change your work week." Or maybe I would offer this thought: "Maybe an experiment for you this week is to pray the Lord's Prayer

There is something about an experiment that is non-threatening, even inviting. I saw many a directed person be open to any experiment that would bring greater intimacy with Christ.

every morning when you wake up. My hope is that it will serve as a reminder to you that God longs to deliver you from temptation." If I ever did give specific direction, it was always couched as an experiment.

It goes without saying that there will be times in life when we are in need of godly counsel. Spiritual direction gives us a means to meet that need within the body of Christ and within the context of spiritual friendships. Spiritual Direction reinforces the truth that there will always be times when we need others to help us hear the voice of God in our lives.

QUESTIONS TO PONDER

Think about a crossroads in your life right now. How might spiritual direction be a benefit to you as you try and discern God's will for your life?

Do you see how the Sticks, Stars, and Signs method of Spiritual Direction releases one from the pressure of being a great counselor or advice giver?

Would you be open to sitting with a Spiritual Director?

For more information about spiritual direction, read: "Sacred Companions: The Gift of Spiritual Friendship & Direction" by David Benner. David Benner is a professor of both spirituality and psychology. He is also a spiritual director and the author of these well-known books: "Spiritual Direction and the Care of Souls", "Surrender to Love", and "Desiring God's Will."

- 11 -
DOUBTING TOWARD JESUS

Immediately the father of the child cried out and said,
"I believe; help my unbelief." ~ Mark 9:24 ESV

"Inquisitiveness and questioning are inevitable parts of the life
of faith. Where there is certainty there is no room for faith."
~ Philip Yancey

It was a beautiful day in San Francisco. By a beautiful day I mean that the fog had lifted, the breeze was light, temperature perfect, humidity low, and the brilliant blue sky was dotted with large puffs of white cloud. On that perfect Bay Area day, a few friends and I had decided to make a day of it in the city. We crossed the bridge, visited the wharf, saw the sea lions, and made our way into the heart of the city to visit an art museum.

The San Francisco Art Museum proved to be a very exciting exercise in culture. There were sculptures, paintings, photographs, and various exhibits. Everything we viewed spanned the wide range of artistic methods; abstract to realism, loud to reflective, provocative to tender. I remember my mind being captivated and stimulated. Something about being surrounded by the expressive creativity of others inspired a sense of creation in me. I remember feeling compelled to bring my ideas and understood truth to life through the medium of art or communication.

Spending the time with friends made the experience all the more special. We shared conversations about what we saw and what we found enriching. I do not know about you, but I think the world has robbed the meaning of the word intimacy. It is been claimed by the lingerie shops and the glamor magazines that line the grocery checkout shelves. However, I feel this word is valuable in the scope of relationships.

Intimacy is not just the cheapened version of physical interaction. No, to me, intimacy is the sum of all shared experiences you have with another. Now, as it pertains to a husband and wife, the role of physical intimacy is surely a portion of that experiential sum. Yet with friends, family, and the church, intimacy is measured in the frequency of quality life moments together. This day in San Francisco was one of those shared moments with friends and the church.

After leaving the art museum, we decided to head to a popular shopping district. My hope was there would be food. My stomach was growling. Upon arriving in the immensely busy bottlenecked intersection, my stomach turned for a different reason. You can just imagine, in downtown San Francisco, what we were looking at. Where your mind goes will say a lot.

Standing on the street corner, with large picket signs, were a group of charismatic preachers. They were waving their Bibles in the air and pronouncing condemnation and judgment on all the passers-by. Their sign read something like: "You're going to Hell." I cannot remember the exact phrasing, but I do remember becoming instantly upset.

Of course, I was initially upset for completely selfish reasons. These men were ruining my beautiful day in the city with friends. Their shouting was annoying and their message, though containing slivers of truth, was delivered in a complete rage versus righteousness way. Some people would ignore them. Others would heckle them, which in turn fed their fiery delivery; since they now had supposedly suffered for the name of Jesus. The whole scene was bothersome.

After my initial frustrations subsided a bit, I discovered I was upset for another reason. If, in fact, these people on the streets of San Francisco were going to hell, was this the best way to tell them? What if these people, deep down in their soul, were craving for what only God could provide? How would they know that hope was something God offered based on the signs they were reading? What if they were not opposed to God, they just did not have all the facts? What if all that stood between these city dwellers and tourists no longer being lost, but found was doubt?

As my brain swarmed with questions, an idea popped into my head. *Why don't I just go up and ask them these very questions?* So I did. For nearly an hour, I spoke with them. I asked them about the good news of their message. I asked them to share the logic behind their strategy. I asked the sign-toting evangelist if he ever saw any real fruit of repentance or transformation as a result of their methods. Finally, I asked if anyone with real doubts about God ever stopped and had a good conversation so encouraging to their soul that they became Christ followers right there on the spot. Their answers were as I expected, *weak*.

People doubt the reality of God because they see little evidence of His power in the world and especially in His followers. They doubt because God seems distant and at times judgmental. They come with questions to the church attending, Bible-believing Christians who have little more than pat answers for some of life's toughest dilemmas. So, unfortunately, nothing feels real or authentic to the wayward children of God.

I think we live in a world full of doubters more than a world of disregarders.

I often think we, as God's church, have approached this evangelism idea the wrong way. We have poured all of our efforts into making people believe, and now. I wonder if it would be okay to let people truly doubt toward Jesus. That may sound strange, but hear me out. What if instead of equipping the church with faith-sharing formulas or Jesus selling techniques, we just showed both lost and found how to listen to God. What if instead of getting people to listen to our clever church marketing, we taught the wayward how to hear the voice of the Lord. The Holy Spirit does the drawing anyway. How about we just help people notice and hear from Him.

The Sticks, Stars, and Signs of Evangelism

Everyone has a story of faith, even if it is not focused on the person of Jesus. Yes, over half of the world may worship a god other than Jesus. However, that does not mean they have not been exposed to truth or do not have a thirst for the spiritual. With that said, maybe the best place to start with people evangelistically is in a conversation loaded with questions.

I feel that many people who have grown up in church are fearful of questions. For whatever reason, questions have become synonymous with disbelief or challenging the truth of the majority. Questions are for clarity. Questions are methods of discovering the truth. I know that sometimes the tone of a question can be aggressive, but it is only a question. It should not shake the peace when an unbeliever asks a question. My high school science teacher never got upset when people asked about the principles and properties of gravity. Nothing a student said would make it untrue. It was simply a question for clarity.

We have to be ready for questions from an unbelieving world. However, for many entrenched church-goers, and even church staff members, conversation with an unbeliever can be a rarity. The insulated walls of church and a hectic ministry schedule have long since separated them from those that need to hear the hope of the gospel.

For many, evangelism will mean altering one's schedule or activities in order to engage unbelievers in conversation and establishing a real friendship. I tell people, when in doubt, take a walk in your neighborhood or linger a little bit longer at the local third place. You will soon find people that need Christ, people with a spiritual curiosity or crisis.

Of course, many church members work with unbelievers, have unbelieving family members, and are immersed in a culture that does not regard Jesus as the highest priority. The first step toward relationship in these settings is also the same, conversation. By conversation, I do not mean a basic chit-chat about the weather or a rundown of the latest sports event either. The point of spiritual conversation is to truly get to know someone's heart. Ask about jobs, spouses, family, hobbies, and even spiritual upbringing. Express a genuine interest in someone, and they will share their lives with you. Conversation is the gateway to the heart of a person.

While having conversations, remember to be an active listener. The more you actively listen, the more something that is spoken will eventually (yes, you guessed it) stick out. There will be a fact or point of interest about your new friend's spiritual background that will make you curious enough to dig for more. With the right amount of time and the right amount of questions, people will always share their thought and doubts about religion, the church, and God Himself.

Keep listening. In time, something will stick out and rise to the surface of conversation.

Some people may be angry at God or the church. Some, with the wrong perspective, might be turned off by the surrender and obedience aspects of faith.

Some will use excuses about not wanting to hang out with a bunch of hypocrites who just want their money. Others might feel they already have a great life and honestly see no need for God or the church.

Be careful in your listening not to act too shocked when someone confesses a sinful past to you. If a friend shares he or she did drugs heavily in their past or have wrestled with homosexual temptations, do not act so surprised that it shuts down the sharing. Remember those sins have been paid for on the cross, and your friend has yet to accept that cleansing gift. Besides, those shocking moments in conversation might stick out to you, but that may not be the actual nugget that God wanted you to notice.

Instead, it could be the heart desire behind those sins is the true piece that sticks out. For example, the drug abuse elements of one's story may be more about one's way of dealing with personal failures. A failed marriage, lost work or dropped friends are problems. But they are symptoms of a greater problem. The real issue may be fear of failure or the relentless shame one feels because of those failures. Either way, be listening and the Lord will lead you to what should stick out.

From Sticks to Stars

When the timing is right, press into the next level of *Sticks, Stars, and Signs*: the emotional level. To do this, I like to ask people "why" questions? Why do they feel they do not need to attend church to be connected? Why do they distrust all pastors? Why do they view church people so badly? Why do they feel religion is a waste of time and energy?

Every single one of those questions has an answer and an emotional reasoning. Many people will answer that they were hurt by the church. Hurt, of course, makes one angry or defensive. Many will express they tried religion as a kid or were forced to attend and now it is just not for them. A track record of seeing zero authenticity or true life transformation among the church can make just about anyone walk away. Still, others will plainly not see a need for faith and dismiss the whole church idea. They just have not witnessed the greatness of God in a way that makes them desperate for Him yet.

The truth is that none of these reasons are truly bad reasons for not attending church, they just need to be deconstructed. People need to realize their doubts are normal and are able to be overcome. Their fears or experiences with the misrepresentation of church can become a bridge to intimacy with Christ, not a roadblock to saving faith. Every single one of these reasons, which represent people, can be opened up and renewed by the Holy Spirit.

One way to delve into the emotional piece with people is to identify with their pain or protest about the church or God Himself. Most of the time when people are sharing, we have a place in our past that does help us relate to them. Use those stories to relate to their story, then press them into God's greater story of redemption.

For example, we could honestly say to our friend, "I used to believe that way about church too when I saw how they treated my mom during her divorce. But ever since attending my current church God has opened my eyes to what the church is supposed to be like. It really has become like a family for me and a lot of that anger or frustration from before is slowly beginning to dissolve."

Another example of identifying with someone might revolve around the idea of past sins and the fear of judgment. You might say something like, "I know you have told me you have had a jaded past, but you have to understand that so many biblical characters and people that fill our pews every Sunday have had the same. There is not one of us that has not done something, said something, or thought something that we and others would not be proud of. But the power of Christ is that He meets us where we are. He is not afraid of your sin, past or present. In fact, He is the only one in history to ever confront sin directly and win—on your behalf."

People need to realize their doubts are normal and are able to be overcome.

Helping people see the beauty of their questions, as long as they are doubting toward the truth of Jesus, is a wonderful moment in any spiritual conversation. The more followers of Christ will allow this style of engagement to take place, the more I believe we will see a lost world embrace the kingdom of heaven.

Yet another means of helping people in the *Stars* emotional portion of the conversation is to ask them this question: "How do you feel God would have looked at or handled your situation?" This can be a powerful question to explore if received properly.

Think of it like this. Let's say you are conversing with a woman who was beaten by her father and verbally abused by her mother. Her emotions may be that of shame over those memories and anger with God that those moments happened to her. What if you carefully asked her to picture one of her worst memories of her mother and father, but this time you asked her to imagine Jesus there with her. Ask her what she thinks Jesus would have said, felt, or even done.

As I have coached these moments with people, I have seen them look at those points of pain in their past quite differently. They now realized that God was just as disappointed, or even more so, at the sinful choices of one person willing to demean and hurt another. Some have seen the righteous anger of Jesus toward their abuser. Some have felt the protective touch of Jesus in that moment. There is something powerful about people realizing they were not alone in hurtful memories of their past. The realization, in turn, helps a victim relate emotionally to God on a much different level than before.

The bottom line is that evangelism is about helping people understand the good news of Jesus. For many people, good news is that Jesus is big enough to handle their emotions, their doubts, and their past while continuing to love them unconditionally. Doubt is not the opposite of faith; that would be fear. I believe Jesus is okay with people's doubts about Him. One way to see it is that doubt is the desire for faith or the hunger for something divinely greater.

Sign Posts for Salvation

When it comes to the "*Signs*" segment of spiritual conversations, there are a few thoughts I would like to give. Of course, the goal for any evangelistic moment is for a person to come to saving faith in Christ. Just like when someone tells you they are getting married or having a baby, that good news calls for congratulations and a time of celebration.

Although the shared good news of Christ is in itself an invitation to salvation, actually calling for the question is not a bad idea either. Knowing when to do just that requires a certain element of sensitivity. I believe the

Anytime the good news of the gospel is shared, it demands a response.

church, with good intentions, can often push seekers into a decision for its sake. The church desires to see salvations and a little pressure never hurt. Right?

Well, pressure can hurt, especially when people tend to avoid pressure sales situations. There is no harm in asking someone if they would like to surrender their lives to Jesus Christ as Lord. But I would encourage you to be sure they are responding to the Lord's invitation through you; His voice, not yours. Trust the counsel of the Holy Spirit. He is the one doing the drawing of souls to Himself. He will not steer you astray.

For unbelievers who seem skeptical of Christians or disillusioned by the church, I would suggest the "Come and See" approach. At the onset of Jesus' ministry, as recorded in the gospel of John, two curious men decide to follow this new rabbi around. Jesus at one point turns to them and asks, "What are you seeking?" They reply to Jesus' question by asking one of their own. "Where are you staying?" they ask. I am not sure that is exactly what they wanted to know, but that is what got asked. Either way, Jesus' answer to them was "Come and see."

Jesus takes two men in a curious and skeptical state and gives them a vague invitation. Come where? There is no destination given. The rabbi's response simply creates more curiosity. See what? Who knows. Jesus does not say, but He does build anticipation that a vision of something new is to be seen if they follow Him. I do not know about you, but I find Jesus' interaction with these men brilliant.

Sometimes the only sign post we need to place on the road to salvation is "Come and See."

It may be that the best invitation you may offer people doubting toward God is "Come and See." For example, a church wounded friend may be hesitant to attend a worship gathering with you and will ask numerous questions about what to expect. Maybe the response simply needs to be, "Come and see." It could be a skeptic might not be too sure sitting in a Lectio gathering is a good idea since they do not believe the Bible to be one hundred percent true. That is when our response should be, "That is okay, just come and see."

Inviting people to an environment where God will reveal Himself to others and through others may be exactly what the unbelieving need. The mystery of the unknown isn't all that bad. See, if we, as the church, define and describe every detail about what friends might expect at a church event, from our perspective, we rob them the joy of making the divine discoveries themselves. Sometimes the only signpost we need to place on the road to salvation is "Come and see." The divine curiosity and the drawing of the Holy Spirit will to the rest.

The final suggestion for offering invitations to unbelievers is confronting mistruths and myths. It is a bit more forceful approach and is very much based on the depth of the relationship one has with a lost friend. There will come moments when challenging people with truth will be needed. Do not ever be afraid to debunk a myth or mistruth about Jesus or His church.

Strong personalities sometimes need an interaction of this intensity to push them into deeper self-reflection. The only caution is to be sure the confronting is about one's false beliefs concerning Christ and His redemptive work. Never confront a person about their personality or their character. Yes, those areas may be abrasive, need attention, or be downright sinful. However, leave that work to Jesus. Do not worry, once they respond to His love and invitation, He will commence with changing the content of their character.

I hope you can now see how *Sticks, Stars, and Signs* can work when ministering to unbelievers and the unchurched. I truly believe this conversational method of evangelism can aid the church in becoming active listeners. Then maybe people will see us as those who care for the lost sons and daughter of God and not the badgers of religiosity.

The more we listen, the more I firmly believe we will help doubters both hear and respond to the voice of the God in their lives. Without fail, that response will begin with salvation and move right into life-long transformation.

QUESTIONS TO PONDER

Who are the people with you whom you have relationship that you know do not have a relationship with Christ?

What are their feelings about God? The church? Heaven and Hell? Life and Death?

What doubts do they have about being a Christian? How can you help your friend's doubt toward God and the truth turn them to Christ instead of away from Him?

How can you use the method of Sticks, Stars, and Signs in evangelism efforts as well?

Commit to engage in a question-based, active listening Sticks, Stars, and Signs conversation this week.

125

Part Three

Vocationally

- 12 -
MY WORK AND MY MISSION

For we are his workmanship, created in Christ Jesus
for good works, which God prepared beforehand, that
we should walk in them. ~ Ephesians 2:10 ESV

"A man knows when he has found his vocation when he stops
thinking about how to live and begins to live." ~ Thomas Merton

My first real job was a paper route. Now I grew up having chores around the house; cleaning, mowing, dishes, and the occasional painting project. But my first real paid gig came in junior high delivering *The Sedalia Democrat* newspaper in central Missouri. At the time I felt it was cool that I had a job. Not many other people that I went to school with actually had real jobs, but to be fair it was junior high. I recall thinking about how I would be rolling in the dough soon. That did not quite happen. I did make some money, but nowhere near enough to roll in. However, what I did gain were quite a few life lessons.

The whole experience became an adventure in character building, from beginning to end. The day I was offered the job, I was riding my bike home from the local grocery store. A car slowly pulled up next to me and a middle-aged man asked me if I lived nearby. Looking back at that moment, it seems pretty creepy. But we lived in a safe, small town. Besides, the world was just a different place in the 1980s.

I told the man, Scott, that I did live close. He went into a sales pitch about how he was looking for teenagers with a desire to work that would be willing to deliver a newspaper on Wednesday afternoons and Sunday mornings. Scott explained the route would have no more than 50 papers and all of the deliveries would be in town. I told him that sounded perfect, but I needed the okay from my parents to seal the deal. Scott followed me home as I rode my bike (that also sounds creepy today). He spoke with my parents and within a few weeks, I was delivering the news.

Wednesdays weren't so bad. I received the papers at my house in the afternoon from a supply car. I would have to roll and rubber band wrap the papers before heading out. With my bag stuffed with cylindrical copies of the news, I would pedal my red ten-speed bike around town tossing papers for an hour or so.

Sundays were a different story. Everything started early and the papers were much bigger thanks to extra advertising inserts, which I also got to stuff in the papers. The supply drop-off happened around 4:30 A.M. The advertisement stuffing and paper rolling would then take about an hour. By 5:30 A.M. I was pedaling. Early mornings in the summer were not all that bad. However, when fall and winter came around, and the weather turned brutally cold, riding a bike outside got rough. I remember doubling my socks and putting my shoes on the heating vent before heading out to combat the conditions.

The route itself was actually pretty fun, at first. I made a game out of trying to get the papers to land perfectly on the porch. At times when I would miss, I would have to dig the paper out of the bushes. One time I even had to retrieve a paper from atop a roof (oops). On the return trip back to my house, I would pass by a home with a horse pasture. I got in the habit of packing an apple or carrots in my bag to feed Mr. Ed, as I called him. We became pretty good friends that summer, Mr. Ed and I.

Certain customers along the route would occasionally talk with me, others would just grumble if the paper was the slightest bit late. I guess people could not function without their daily dose of mostly trivial news. It is funny to think about delivering papers now in our world of technology. I recently heard a comedian describe newspapers as pieces of the internet delivered to your door twenty to thirty pages at a time. Yet, before the internet and twitter, hot off the press still meant something, and I was the kid who delivered the data.

The job eventually ended on a downer, and not just for me. I was told that Scott was stealing money from me and the paper. I wasn't the best accountant as you might now guess. I knew customer collections were not adding up; however, I did not realize Scott was skimming. The paper soon became more of a burden than a blessing and so I retired from the delivery business. That was my introduction into the world of work for pay.

Work: Love It and Loathe It

Work in America is both a cuss word and an addiction. We both love and loathe it. Yes, it pays the bills, but it also comes with a considerable stress connection as well. We want the financial reward it brings, but the time it takes often makes us question the whole system. Is it worth it? Why does it consume so much time? Is a workload like this right or biblical?

During a collegiate mission trip to Pretoria, South Africa, I recall peering out the window of our mini-van at the plethora of roadside vendors selling everything from fruit to clothing. One vendor was packing up his road-side stand at around 10 a.m. I pointed it out and asked why he was leaving so early in the day. Our missionary friend and guide explained that many believe that if they are able to sell what is needed to live on that day, then work is over for that day. It is a mentality of: "Make less money, but live much more."

Although that subsistent lifestyle seemed irresponsible at the time, the freedom and confidence that particular man exuded has haunted me. Work, for him, was a bridge to what was simply needed, not a shackle to which he was ruthlessly bound. Food and shelter were his priorities, not boats and investment properties.

On the flip side, millions upon millions of people are addicted to their work. Work becomes a source of identity, significance, and success. People will arrive early, stay late, work weekends, and take calls during family time and children's ball games in an effort to feed their addiction. It is a strange sickness.

Some would argue that work addicts are in it for the money. I would argue money is a by-product. The real reward for so many is not the income because the addiction exists in the lower middle-class as well. I think the real addition is the feeling of acceptance and "needed-ness" that is generated in the work. The deceptive thoughts of "I am needed, I am wanted, and I am important" continue to feed the addict's fire. That is why a layoff or firing is more about not being wanted than it is about losing income for so many.

Americans are addicted to work. We are near the top of the list for the most worked country in the world. According to the Center for American Progress, 134 countries in the world have laws that set a maximum length for the work week. However, in the United

States research shows that 85.8 percent of males and 66.5 percent of females work more than forty hours per week. The International Labor Organization reports that "Americans work 137 more hours per year than Japanese workers, 260 more hours per year than British workers, and 499 more hours per year than French workers." It is plain to see that we may be a little too connected to our work.[3]

The Huffington Post recent published an article about a syndrome called the "martyr complex." Many work addicted-Americans refuse to take a vacation for fear that no one will do their job as well as them. The mentality of the hyper-driven pushes them to be the best, succeed the most, and rise to the "top of the heap." But what happens when the summit it reached? Satisfaction can never be found at the peak of work-related sacrifice because in time someone else will work harder or smarter. The desperate climb to the heap's top never stops.

Gardener Needed, Baby on the Way

Work may be avoided or abused, but spiritually speaking work was given to us by God. It happened in the Garden of Eden even; before the fall. The work that God gave did not seem all that bad. In the very first chapter of Genesis, Adam and Eve are instructed to be fruitful and multiply. That seems doable. Then right on the heels of that enjoyable decree is a piece about subduing the land, along with caring for the plants and animals. Subduing doesn't sound too laborious either.

I picture Adam naming the animals, a very unique and fun task for the first fledgling human. Now some of the names I get and some of them we might have to ask Adam about. It will be fun one day to ask him about his tending of the Garden. The age old questions to ask Adam, "Did you have to keep certain animals from eating each other? Did you have to mow the grass or trim the bushes or did God maintain the yard work? Were there snakes with legs? Did you kill the creepy crawly spiders or are they post-fall punishment?" Adam punched the clock and got the work done. He

---

[3] http://20somethingfinance.com/american-hours-worked-productivity-vacation/

had dominion over the fish and the birds, every land animal, and all the plants God had placed on the earth. That was Adam's work.

We may look at the story of Adam and his early work career and say, "He does not even understand work. That is such a cushy job. I would love to name animals and look after some plants." However, we have to remember that Adam is the only man to experience work before and after the fall. He and Eve alone are the only two people ever to know the pure joy of God-given work without the penalty of sin's curse upon it.

Remember back to Genesis 3 for a minute. When God is doling out punishment for sin during the fall of man, do you recall the sentences that are given? To the deceiver, the serpent, he makes him the cursed creature of the animal kingdom. Enmity, a state of constant opposition and hostility, is the word that God uses to describe the relationship between man and the serpent, the devil.

Simply put, because of that moment we are always at war with Satan, the accuser of the saints. Greater still, Satan's punishment is incomplete. His greatest destruction is yet to come. In other words, thankfully, one day all enmity and war will be over when Satan is vanquished forever. His work will end; God's work will endure forever.

The punishments rendered to Adam and Eve are fairly unique in that it affected their work immensely. Eve was sentenced with the pains of childbirth. I imagine that if it were not for the splendor of Jesus in heaven, Eve might get a severe tongue-lashing from every woman arriving in paradise. The pain placed on childbirth directly affected the work of Eve to be fruitful and multiply. In addition to the physical pain now associated with bringing forth life, God rendered that woman would play a godly submissive role to man from that day on. We see how misunderstood and divisive that work has been in our culture, our world.

The penalty given to Adam was distinctive to his line of work as well. God says that because the man sinned in the eating of the fruit, the ground he was called to care for would now be cursed. There was work, but now there were thorns and thistles as well. Fruits and vegetables provided by God to man would now face resistance from the very soil in which they were planted. Plants tended to so easily before now required great sweat and toil to manage. The very wonder of the work Adam was given by God before would now be wrought with weeds and weariness.

Isn't that what work feels like to you all too often? Don't you often feel weary over your work? Not only can the curse of sin be felt in child-bearing, but also in the difficulties of child-rearing as well. So much of the work of our hands can feel like pulling weeds only to see them return time and time again. So much of the toil and sweat of our brow does not come with a sense of real joy and pleasure. The work we have been given has been plagued with the weeds of our human infidelity to God.

What if we could recapture the heart of our divine work?

What if we could learn to recognize the weeds
from the real work God has given us to do?

What if work was a place we found mission and joy
because we lived as though it were God-given?

I believe this can be true of us today because it has been true of my journey as it pertains to work.

Ministry as Work

After my paperboy days were far behind I bounced back and forth between job ideas. At one point I wanted to be a computer programmer, then a history teacher and coach, and ultimately I left for college to become a lawyer. Despite my big plans, God had a bit more in store for me during that first year away at school.

After graduating from a small high school in Southern Illinois, I attended Union University in Jackson, Tennessee. Now this was a big step for me, not only because it was four hours from home, but because it was in the South. I had never really been to the South before college. Sure, my family and I took a trip to the Ozarks and Branson, Missouri, but I thought that hillbilly stuff was just for the tourist. I was wrong.

Being a Yankee and a Midwesterner all of my life, I experienced a great deal of culture-shock in Tennessee. I can still remember my first social function with some of the college students I had just met. It was a church get-together at the pastor's house for a fellowship meal. When I arrived I was told we would be eating barbecue. However, when I saw the grill on the back porch patio, it was covered. Then they proceeded to pull out foil trays containing barbecued pork meat. That was not the barbecue of which I was familiar. As a kid, I watched my dad grill everything over a charcoal fire. That was barbecue. Besides, the only time we used foil was if something actually made it to the leftover phase.

I was then asked about football and if I was a fan of the University of Tennessee Volunteers. Now you have to understand that I am a huge football fan, but in the North and Midwest in the 1980s and 90s it was all about pro ball. I grew up, and still am, a diehard Buffalo Bills fan. Watching Jim Kelly, Thurman Thomas, and Andre Reed operate the K-Gun no huddle offense was a thrill.

So when I was asked about college football, the only team I really even paid any attention to in the college realm was the Florida Gators. The Gators had an explosive offense, much like my Bills. So, over my foil covered meat, I responded to the question about the Volunteers with, "I kind of like the Gators offense." Bad decision. SEC Madness ensued. Culture shock again took over.

College itself was a shock in that I actually had to study and open a book; something I did not do much of in high school. My workload shocked me, the teacher's wisdom and challenges shocked me, my roommates shocked me, and even the diversity of the city I was living in shocked me. In fact, there was not much that did not shock me and wake me up to a whole new world during my freshmen year away at Union. So you can only imagine how I felt when the Lord decided to shock me as well. The one place that I wanted freedom from shock and awe was with God. Yet, if you have followed Christ for any length of time, or you have read the Scriptures, then you know shock is kind of His thing.

One day, during my first spring semester, while sitting in my political science class, God began to speak. This was a class I both loved and hated. Dr. Ann Livingston was a fierce and challenging professor. She loved the political realm and felt everyone should understand the beauty and disgust of the world's political systems. She pressed every small town conservative button I had, multiple times, but she did it in a caring and motivating way. Dr. Livingston stretched my mind enough to see the world from different angles, and for that, I am profoundly grateful.

The day God shocked me about my future work, I remember sitting in the back row of the classroom as Dr. Livingston lectured passionately. It was a topic I was interested in, or at least I thought I was. However, that day, for whatever reason, all my passion and desire for this topic, this classroom moment, and even my chosen life course seemed to drain out of me like water from a bathtub. I felt empty, confused, and very concerned. I left class feeling low, but the trip to the dorm brought a whole new dynamic to my feelings.

To this day, I can remember the Lord saying to me, *"This is not what I have for you."*

The rest of the conversation, though condensed for your enjoyment, went a *little* like this *(Note: God and I speak bluntly)*:

"This is not what I have for you," He said.

"This is NOT what you have for me Lord?"

"No. I have greater things in store for you."

"Oh, really? Do you think that might be something I should have known before I was about to wrap up my freshmen year? Do you think that would have been nice to know when I was praying for wisdom while in high school? Do you think that would have been a good piece of information to have before I left my home, four hours away, to attend a university that costs a ton, where I am slaving away at two jobs to make it happen? God, I cannot afford to waste my time and money because you have an idea. What is the greater things you have for me?"

"I want you to work with the generation behind you. I want to use you as a tool to awaken people to a grander view of me. I made you and have crafted you in such a way that you can make an impact for me in my kingdom."

"Well, that is great God. I can make an impact on the youth generation behind me by being a Sunday School teacher on Sundays. I could even host a few youth group events at my nice house as a lawyer. Sound like a plan?"

"Not exactly. I want you to let go of all the work you wanted to do and do my work. Trust me, it is better to work."

"But my dad is a pastor. Isn't one pastor in the family enough?"

(No answer.)

"Okay, so that means I am not going to be a lawyer?"

"Yes."

"That means I need to change my major and school focus?"

"Yes."

"That means I won't be rich one day?"

"A different kind of rich."

I would like to say that my initial invitation from God was enough for me to surrender on the spot and change course. But the wrestling continued on for a few months before I surrendered to the ministry. Now I use the phrase "surrender to the ministry" only to describe my vocational reorientation. I do not like that phrase because I think it lets many "lay people" off the hook. People can easily say, "Well, I am not surrendered to the ministry."

When you lay down your life to take up Christ's life, you are now surrendered to the ministry. You can argue with me all day long about the significance of a full-time call to pastoring. Trust me, I understand it is distinctive. However, I am simply arguing for a bigger perspective on the matter.

The truth is that all who are in Christ have surrendered to the ministry.

Everyone is called to serve God in the secular and sacred work of their life. Vocationally speaking, some are granted the opportunity to make a living as professional pastors or missionaries. But just to be clear, whether a pastor or park ranger, all are called to the ministry of making an eternal kingdom impact.

As my calling became more and more clear, I shared my heart with Michelle (my near fiancée at the time), my family, and my church. Everyone had their own thoughts or advice about my coming transition. I heard everything from "You will be poor" to "I knew it! Praise the Lord!" The pastor of the local church I attended helped guide me, Union University did its best to educate me, and my dad and mom gave me words of encouragement from their current tenure in full-time ministry. But the greatest encouragement during that time came from God through the writings of the prophet Jeremiah.

Now the word of the Lord came to me, saying, "Before I formed you in the womb I knew you, and before you were born I consecrated you; I appointed you a prophet to the nations." Then I said, "Ah, Lord God! Behold, I do not know how to speak, for I am only a youth." But the Lord said to me, "Do not say, 'I am only a youth'; for to all to whom I send you, you shall go, and whatever I command you, you shall speak. Do not be afraid of them, for I am with you to deliver you, declares the Lord."

Then the Lord put out his hand and touched my mouth.
And the Lord said to me, "Behold, I have put my words in your
mouth. See, I have set you this day over nations and over
kingdoms, to pluck up and to break down, to destroy and to
overthrow, to build and to plant."

~ Jeremiah 1:4-10 ESV emphasis added

Formed in the Womb

When I read those words, I felt the calling of God in my soul deeper than before. My life, in that moment, was much like that of Jeremiah the prophet. I was young. I had a story that assured me I was set apart by the Lord from birth, and now God had appointed me to be a minister to the nations.

My mother and biological father were not followers of Christ when they first met and decided to marry. As one might imagine, a life and a marriage without Christ as the focus can easily unravel. Before long my mother found herself pregnant with a big choice on her hands. Would she do what was needed to be the mother she needed to be? Greater still, would her baby's physical health be okay? See doctors were telling her that because of recreational drug issues, I could possibly be a drug baby with long-term health issues. She was even encouraged to consider abortion as an early term option.

As might be more than obvious now, my mother did the holy thing in preserving life and raising her newborn with all her heart and energy. I identified with Jeremiah. Just as he was set apart by God from birth, so was I. Plus, I was now embracing the deeper purpose for which God had created me.

There is something within each of us that craves to know the deeper reason we were created. People can deny that desire or distract themselves with lesser purposes or worldly pleasures, but in the quiet moments of the night, when doubts and fears arise, those cravings will resurface. For me, at the age of nineteen, I now had a piece of my future purpose revealed. The feeling of God appointing me to a specific mission was truly amazing. In many ways, that was one of the most marvelous moments of my life.

Youth is a precious thing. I am approaching thirty-nine, which is the gateway to a life in the forties. Some of you may be reading this and say, "Oh to be forty again." However, I am not there so allow me a little latitude to moan a bit. Nineteen seems so long ago, a truth of which I am reminded of every time I play full-court basketball and attempt to get out of bed the next day. I don't know about you, but I am starting to think that gravity is especially strong in the morning. I know it won't get any better, it's just that I am starting to embrace the reality that I am not as young as I used to be.

Odd enough, when I was younger I had a lot more knowledge. Have you ever realized that? If you were to ask me anything when I was 19, I had the answer. However, the last twenty years have caused me to realize how much I do not actually know. I think that is the joy of maturing, you come to peace with the fact that life can often be filled with more profound questions than real answers. It is a challenge to the structure of faith that forces one's spiritual roots to plunge deeper and deeper into the mystery of God.

At nineteen, what did I know? Less than I thought I did. At nineteen, what could I do to have kingdom impact on others? What could I say that could help change a life? Not much, but the Spirit of God coursing through my veins was ready to accomplish much.

The more I embraced and understood my calling, the more I found myself identifying with Jeremiah. At times I questioned God, wanted to throw in the towel, or even felt the pressure of enemies against the move of God in my life and others. However, without fail, I would return to that place of calling on my life. Even today, I never doubt that God has a calling on my life. I know it because I have heard Him speak it over and over again.

QUESTIONS TO PONDER

Using the *Sticks, Stars, and Signs* method of listening to God through the scriptures, engage with Him with the Jeremiah text below. Take your time and meditate on what sticks out, how this passage stirs your emotions, and what step of faith Jesus is asking you to take today. What might God be saying to you about work and mission through this passage? Enjoy.

> *Now the word of the Lord came to me, saying, "Before I formed you in the womb I knew you, and before you were born I consecrated you; I appointed you a prophet to the nations." Then I said, "Ah, Lord God! Behold, I do not know how to speak, for I am only a youth." But the Lord said to me, "Do not say, 'I am only a youth'; for to all to whom I send you, you shall go, and whatever I command you, you shall speak. Do not be afraid of them, for I am with you to deliver you, declares the Lord."*
>
> *Then the Lord put out his hand and touched my mouth. And the Lord said to me, "Behold, I have put my words in your mouth. See, I have set you this day over nations and over kingdoms, to pluck up and to break down, to destroy and to overthrow, to build and to plant."*
>
> ~ *Jeremiah 1:4-10 ESV*

— Sticks

* Stars

> Signs

- 13 -
SIXTEEN YEARS AND ALL WAS WELL

If I say, "I will not mention him, or speak any more in his name," there is in my heart as it were a burning fire shut up in my bones, and I am weary with holding it in, and I cannot. ~ Jeremiah 20:9 ESV

"Your identity is firmly anchored in Christ's accomplishment, not yours; his strength, not yours; his performance, not yours; his victory, not yours. Your identity is steadfastly established in his substitution, not in your sin." ~ Tullian Tchividjian

Over time it happened. Well, it took sixteen years, but it happened. What happened you may ask? To put it simply, a calling became work. A pursuit of God's eternal kingdom became clouded by the professional pastorate position, a job title. The joy of God's people forged together by the common thread of Christ's glorious resurrection slowly was superseded by the machine of church and church growth. The natural eroding descent back to a lesser plan for life than the one God had given had taken place.

Some of you may read that last paragraph and you may think it sounds completely cold and detached from the real purpose and passion of the everyday pastor. Let me clue you in. Not every minute is like a fish fry for five thousand on a mountain or conquering Jericho with the jazz band. If your pastor has led you to believe that, I would venture to say he is hiding his pain from you. Every pastor I have known goes through moments when church feels like work and ministry feels the farthest thing from a calling.

If I am honest, there were moments during my sixteen years as a full-time pastor that "my calling" erosion took place, but nothing as drastic at what happened in year fifteen. That is when God began to speak into my calling with yet another shock and awe moment. This shocking moment scared me more than any other. It humbled me, frightened me, angered me, and changed my perception of work forever. Let me explain.

In the spring of 2011, I remember leaving a church staff meeting with a sense of bewilderment. It was the same loss and confusion that I had first experienced during my days in Dr. Livingston's political science class. All the passion for what I was doing presently was suddenly gone again.

I had been working for the past five years as a pastor of college and young adults in a respected church in the Central Valley of California. God had given me a wonderful opportunity to invest in a specific demographic of Christ-followers. Helping young people at the very crossroads of their life, relationally and vocationally, was truly a blessing. It was thrilling to see them become a catalyst for change for the kingdom of heaven right before my eyes. But things were suddenly different.

Being a part of a larger church staff has its pros and cons. When it came to pros, there was not a week that went by that I was not astounded and blessed by another member of our ministry team. That is not to mention the leadership skills and wisdom I gleaned from my fellow staff members. The collaborative projects at Christmas, though somewhat stressful, were deeply impacting moments. The teamwork, togetherness, and collective talents used in declaring the gospel story was remarkable.

Plus there were top-notch guest speakers that would come and share at our church. I will never forget sitting with Dan Allender over breakfast and picking his brain after he had spoken at one of our church events the night before. It was remarkable. His wisdom and perceptiveness about life and deep matters truly amazed me.

The negatives or "con's" of larger church environments, for me, were the amount of time-consuming meetings, the wonder of office bureaucracy, and the strong expectations toward accomplishment. Growth was desired but the pacing for growth was not always gauged fairly. Additionally, in larger organizations, policies and business models tend to rule. This is not because they are evil or wrong, but because they are needed and effective. However, when you sit through one too many meetings about growth expectation and organizational strategies, you can tend to lose the joy and purpose behind the reason you are employed at all.

On one such day, after a slew of meetings, I remember sitting in my office thinking about the early church and if Peter and the gang struggled with the fatigue and dissonance that I felt. That is when God began to speak to my heart. However, what He said challenged me deeper than ever before. I know I am a whiner about meetings and church models at times, but God took things a little too far that day. I clearly remember him saying, "I want you to resign, and not get paid for ministry."

The Beginning and the End

Resigning and leaving a church was something that had happened in my life before. It was not ever my desire. I am a very loyal person, so to leave any place for another, whether I love it or not, is difficult for me. But this was not what God was asking of me. He was not asking me to simply resign; he was asking me not to get paid for doing the work of the ministry. That was not okay with me at all.

I had heard about people who did not get paid to do ministry but worked bi-vocational instead. They were, of course, poor, religiously crazy, missionaries on the foreign field or all three. How could I get paid to do anything else? I was not trained or equipped to do anything else. I surrendered any possible means of money-making in college to become a pastor. The list of reasons of why I could not quit just kept growing.

My kids were in private school. We had good insurance. Life was fairly comfortable on a lot of levels. The church was great, despite my loathing the meetings at times. I had a family to support. What was God thinking? Had he gone crazy? There was no way this idea would work at all. I chalked the moment to a trying day at work or bad tacos for lunch and tried to forget it happened. However, my attempt at blind ignorance did not last too long.

If you have or have had little children, you know that moment when you tell them, "Just a minute," and they pester you non-stop until you finally meet their need or give them the proper attention. For the next month, it was like I had told God, "Just a minute." He would not let this idea of ministry without pay just disappear.

After a bit of panic and confusing prayer moments, I went and spoke with Jon about what I heard the Lord was saying to me. I needed spiritual direction. He was good to push me back to the Lord. Jon is always good to do that. He consistently asks everyone he sits with, "What have you heard the Lord saying to you in the midst of this situation?" He is a firm believer in the fact that we must truly learn to listen to the voice of God in all situations; a truth I am glad I have gleaned from him.

The more I spoke with God about it, the more I began to swallow the truth that I was being asked to leave everything I had known as a career for the last fifteen years. The next step was to bring the idea to my wife, Michelle. She was surprisingly okay with it. She was very encouraging to me about the process I was in. From that day on we were trying to determine what God had spoken to us and what that meant for our family long term.

By the summer of 2011, I had reached a place of peace about the next chapter of my life being one where I was not going to be working full-time for a local church. To be fair, that decision was made in my mind by that summer, but it took time for my heart and life to really wrap around it. Even writing that sentence now takes me back to that season of fear and reluctance.

Firsts and Lasts

Soon after Michelle and I committed to taking this next step in life, I left for a collegiate mission trip to South Africa. The reality of what God was asking me to surrender was super fresh on my mind. When God invites us to obedience, it is not always the easiest or the most desired step—as we talked about in earlier chapters. However, obedience is always the correct step.

I recall sitting in the living room of the mission compound, looking at the team God had assembled for that year. I have been on a lot of mission trips, but that specific team was extremely special. The Lord had truly knit us together in heart and mind. One specific night of team debriefing turned into an emotional overflow for me as I praised each person for how I saw God at work in them and how they were a blessing to me. I knew I would not be leading mission teams like that anytime soon in the future. I had already begun grieving the loss of a job of which I had not officially resigned.

The rest of the year was the beginning of a lot of lasts. It would be the last Christmas presentation in California, the last College and Young Adult retreat to Mount Hermon, and the last time my job title would have pastor in it, at least for a time. There was much to which I would slowly need to say good-bye, even up to the day that I actually resigned from my position at the church.

Of course, the year ahead was also filled with a lot of firsts, too. It would be the first time I would look for full-time employment outside of a church. It would also be the first time that my wife would make more money than me. I would like to say that never once made me feel funny, but that is not quite the case. Though I was thankful for income, it did challenge my manliness a bit.

It was the first time that I would start my own business. It was the first time in a while that people hesitantly congratulated me about my work and life decision. People at the church even took me aside to be sure I had truly heard from God. I assured them I had and I was trusting in Him for provision and guidance. That was completely the case, although some days I could answer with a bit more confidence.

When I resigned, neither Michelle nor I had jobs. We did not know where we would live, even though we assumed we would move back to the Knoxville area where Michelle grew up. Additionally, we did not know where we would worship, where the kids would attend school, or even if we could afford anything but a small apartment for the four of us and the dog. Trust was all we had.

Tennessee Bound

The months ticked by quickly after my decision to resign from full-time ministry. The church was gracious to let me stay on until our kiddos finished out the year at the private school, which was an educational ministry of the church. My daughter was graduating eighth grade, my son completing fifth. The day after her graduation, we loaded up the moving van and the cross-country trek began.

In the days leading up to our move, God had shown his provision in powerful ways. Michelle got a great job with a hospice agency in a town near our new home just south of Knoxville, Tennessee. The kids had come to terms with entering a public high school and middle school, and I had found myself adjusting slowly to entering a new career path.

I have long loved fitness and cycling as hobbies. Near the end of my stay in California, I was working at a gym for fun on my off hours from church. To be honest, it was a great way to meet unchurched people and make new relationships. With my first career path taken off the table, I decided to pursue work in the fitness field and became a certified personal trainer.

It is one thing to have worked sixteen years at a profession and slowly climb a ladder of responsibility and leadership. However, starting a new career means starting over at the bottom rung of the ladder. That was not something I found easy at all. My business started slow and each step challenged my trust in God's voice and His invitation on my life. Without a doubt, I was humbled by the whole transition.

Before long, God had proven Himself faithful and clients were coming. Now, I would not say that I have hit the big time financially in the fitness field, but I would say that we are eating dinner nightly, and my new job has changed my views on work and ministry as a lay person.

New Perspectives

When it came to work, I quickly realized that my identity was strongly connected to my job title at church. It was difficult to separate who I was from what I did. Who was I if I was not a pastor at so and so church? There is something in us, especially men, that allows us, even craves, to be identified by what we produce or do.

Alan Fadling, a friend and author of "An Unhurried Life", helped me see this identity piece much clearer one day. He was speaking to a group about the command to honor the Sabbath. As he shared, he drove home the point that the people of Israel, after being enslaved for some 400 years, actually had to be commanded to rest. Their bondage to and their work for the Egyptians had so shaped their identity they needed to be forced to stop and be still. On that day of rest, the Sabbath, God would remind His people who they were. Their identity could only be established by Yahweh.

Unraveling my identity from my work and being sure it was defined by Christ alone took work.

Spending my first summer of Sabbath in Tennessee, while trying to undo my work and identity misunderstandings, was emotionally difficult. I wrestled with apathy, depression, and a general sense of confusion. Sadly, I felt as though my worth as a man was lessened. I am a decent trainer I think, but I am a better pastor. For sixteen years I had built up my experience as a pastor and honed my craft. The very thing I felt I was good at I was not doing. Part of me even felt like God put me on the shelf for a while so He could play with other toys. It was a difficult summer.

We attended new churches, and as much as I did enjoy being a lay person with no responsibility at times, it was difficult to also remain in the background. I am a leader in a lot of ways and I enjoy leading from the front of the room. I cannot explain just how fidgety I was in church. Every bit of me wanted to jump up and tag the pastor and say, "Okay, my turn. I got this." That may work in wrestling, but it does not work in the church.

I remember calling a local denominational headquarters near my home one day. My hope was to be put on a list for supply preaching if any churches in the area needed temporary fill-ins or interim work. The man on the phone questioned me a bit and laughed off my request when He realized I worked in a non-denominational church in California. His comment to me was, "People may wonder what was wrong, and why did you leave our family of churches?"

Really, I thought. *What was wrong?* That phone call severely angered me. For the record, my wife told me not to make it. I have since told her she was right, begrudgingly of course. Needless to say, that first summer in Tennessee was a struggle. In many ways, I felt like something was wrong with me. What was wrong was I listened to God.

Please understand, I say that lightly. I knew God had me where He wanted me. Just learning to let go of who I was and let God establish my identity apart from my work alone was challenging. Becoming a lay person who serves from a place of pure passion versus for a paycheck has actually been liberating. Some days I cannot imagine working solely for a church anymore. The desire to be on staff at a church occasionally crops up, but I have learned to deal with those desires in a much godlier manner now.

To be clear, I am not arguing that you cannot or should not be a full-time paid pastor in a church and serve God. I am simply sharing how the Lord has invited me to be obedient. With that said, let's examine a bit more the idea of work and ministry in the Scriptures.

QUESTIONS TO PONDER

What is the calling of God on your life? Do you know it? Have you heard Him speak it over you? How is your identity being shaped by His call on you to work and mission?

What is your idea of work?

What are your thoughts on a lifestyle of ministry versus ministry as a career or job?

How can you embrace the calling to be a pastor and a priest, no matter what work you do?

- 14 -
HOW JESUS WORKED

*And Jesus increased in wisdom and in stature
and in favor with God and man. ~ Luke 2:52 ESV*

*"Let every man abide in the calling wherein he is called
and his work will be as sacred as the work of the ministry.
It is not what a man does that determines whether
his work is sacred or secular, it is why he does it." ~ A.W. Tozer*

When you look at the life of Jesus in the Scriptures you quickly realize that His work was not always that of full-time Rabbi. Jesus spent the vast majority of His life being a carpenter like His father, Joseph. It was not until He turned thirty that Jesus even began what we would call His public ministry. So the question becomes, before Jesus entered into His sacred calling on the earth, was the rest of His work secular?

Would we say that the tables Jesus made were simply secular work and one would hope that He found time to serve at the local synagogue as well? Would we argue that His time spent building a temporal home probably distracted Him from building our eternal homes in heaven? Was His sacred calling only found in His role as rabbi or could His carpentry work be considered sacred as well? If you want to argue those points, then go ahead. Something in me does not quite feel that bold.

What I am trying to highlight is our polarizing view about work and ministry in the church. My experiences in the church have shaped how I look at work. Yes, most of the people who attend church on Sundays work a "secular job" during the week. It's just that I was subtly taught that their ministry efforts were only accomplished while at church.

It might help to see it this way. Joe may be a plumber Monday-Saturday, but on Sunday, he is a discipleship class teacher (unless the baptismal was leaking. Then he was a plumber again). Sherry may be a first-grade teacher during the week, but on the weekend her ministry to the body was fulfilled as the church's nursery coordinator. Businessman Bob owned and managed multiple businesses during the week, but on Sunday he was the church's offering counter and bookkeeper.

Do you see the parody created by this view of work and ministry? Just as much as I could confidently say that Jesus saw everything He did as a means to glorify God and expand the reign of His earthly kingdom, I believe we need to adopt a lifestyle view of ministry.

That may sound like semantics, but it is truly not. When Joe the plumber sees his work as ministry just like his discipleship class, then repairing the broken pipes in people's homes becomes an invitation to repair the same people's broken relationships with God. When Sherry sees her school classroom as a place to let the little children come unto Jesus as much as her nursery on Sunday, she has adopted a lifestyle of ministry. When Bob has the opportunity to teach and demonstrate biblical principles of finance and ethics to his colleagues and employees, then Bob realizes work is his ministry.

> *Ministry is first and foremost a lifestyle before it is ever a career.*

Though it seems like the simple flipping of a switch in our heads to make this mindset a reality, it has actually taken quite a bit of focus for me. Even now when training people at the gym, I can slip into "trainer-only" mode and forget the "personal-care" piece. The body needs training, but I must remember how I can be fully present to my clients in order to be a blessing to their souls as well.

All too often in the church, I think we have created a great divide between the lay person and the pastor. If you stand on the platform, then you're in ministry. But if you're seated in the pew, then you need to find a ministry in the church soon.

Here's a radical thought:

> *What if we empowered every person in the church to see themselves as part of the pastoral staff?*

How would that change the impact of our church on the community in which we live?"

If the pastor is the only teacher, then people must attend the church building to hear truth. But if every member is taught to see themselves as a bearer of truth, then when the church scatters into the marketplace during the week, truth scatters like seeds in good soil as well. If the worship leader is the only one who leads people to praise God, then people must wait for his leadership on Sunday from the platform to glorify God. But if everyone saw themselves as lead worshipers, scattered into the workplace, how much more would the name of God be lifted high in all the earth.

Pastors have to be careful not to make people so dependent on them for ministry to happen. We are not the dispensers of grace, God is. The last I checked God can use anyone to do His work, even talking donkeys. I think that is why in Exodus 19:6 Yahweh reminds Moses that He is making for Himself a kingdom of priests. The word priest in this verse is plural for a reason. The expectation of Yahweh is that everyone who makes up the nation of Israel will take on the role of connecting family and foreigner with the God that so powerfully rescued them from Egypt.

Imagine if churches today implanted that level of missional expectancy in their church membership. You want to rid the church of consumerism, tell congregants they are expected to be priests in their homes and workplaces every day of the week; connecting the wayward to their Heavenly Father. Then teach them how to listen to God and guide them to help others do the same. Nothing will connect people to God faster than teaching the church to listen for the God's voice and then share His truth with others.

Serving as long as I did as a pastor, I quickly realized how much people avoid pastors like they avoid car salesman and the perfume squirters at the mall. However, people do not seem to run from photographers and realtors. They may hate dentists and personal trainers, but for different reasons.

Everyday professions staffed by saints that view themselves as pastors and priests flips the whole missionary model upside down. Work is an excuse to be on a mission for the kingdom while you make enough money to buy dinner and pay off your house. I truly believe that in today's world, the kingdom needs more surrendered saints than it does polished professionals.

Paul's words to the Ephesians come to mind when I think about the church scattered at work all week long. He writes: "For we are his workmanship, created in Christ Jesus for good works, which God prepared beforehand, that we should walk in them" (Ephesians 2:10 ESV). That is a great description of ministry as a lifestyle and work as an opportunity to minister. God has made *you* His work that you may do *His* work in the world; work prepared for you since before time began.

Leading From the Front Again

About one year after moving to Tennessee, our family stumbled on a church plant which we quickly connected with its heart. For the whole first year, we had bounced around a few places, but never really found our niche or felt a peace about staying. Yet this church plant had an organic nature to their ministry methods and a heart for true discipleship and life transformation. We sensed God at work, and even more so, we sensed we were to join in the work.

Not long after our decision to join, I approached the pastors and shared with them my background and my heart. Yes, I did type pastors. The church plant was then being led by two bi-vocational pastors. Both of the leaders were tent-makers like myself who had felt God's call to plant a church in the same area of Knoxville.

Over coffee, I shared with these guys that I was trying to serve the Lord as a trainer and if they could use my ministry heart and skills I wanted to be a blessing to them. I offered to be an Aaron and a Hur to them, as one willing to lift up their arms in support of what they were doing for God's kingdom. They accepted the help and the partnership began.

Ministry as a lifestyle is still my focus, but it has also been fun that God has allowed me to lead from the front again. I have had the privilege of preaching and teaching again, which I believe is how the Spirit has gifted me. There have been other means by which God has used me in this congregation, but I am mostly just glad to be with people who understand that ministry is more than titles, resumes, or trying to be the most popular church on the block. We truly have a passion to shepherd the people of God and to be a missional presence in our community.

I do not know if I will ever be a full-time paid staff member at a church again. I have learned not to rule out anything with God. For now, I am thankful that I obeyed that initial call to resign. I cannot imagine all the maturing moments I would have missed had I stayed. One thing is for sure, this book would not have come to fruition had I neglected God's call to obedience. I'm glad I chose to have ears to listen and the faith to respond.

QUESTIONS TO PONDER

Using the framework of Sticks, Stars, and Signs, evaluate what you do for a living.

STICKS: What sticks out to you about your work? What do you love? What do you dislike?

STARS: What work do you feel emotionally drawn to? What would you do for work if money were no issue? How can God use that desire to shape your future?

SIGNS: What invitations are you hearing from God about your workplace? What is He asking you to surrender? Where is obedience to Him a challenge?

- 15 -
THE CHURCH:
WHAT IF WE QUIT LISTENING?

Doing something for you, bringing something to you—
that's not what you're after. Being religious, acting pious—
that's not what you're asking for. You've opened my ears
so I can listen. ~ Psalm 40:6 MSG

"Big egos have little ears."
~ Robert Schuller

I remember being a kid, and it was fun. I know that sounds somewhat obvious and pretty ridiculous, but it is true. Days at school were filled with learning and laughter. Occasionally there was a scuffle or the random rude remarks, but for the most part, we got along. We played kickball, four-square, or just sat around and talked at recess. The biggest worry was whether or not we would have a quiz in science.

After school, I walked the half mile home. I did not worry about whether or not I would get kidnaped or be sold crack. The door to my house was usually unlocked. Sometimes mom or dad were home, but if they were not they left a note. Afternoons were not consumed with loads of homework, but play. On pretty days, I would break out the bike or toss the ball in our side yard. School days were pretty simple.

When it came to summer breaks or holidays, things got even better. We would have so much free time to ride bikes, explore the woods, swim, and play ball. Small town summer sports consisted of little league baseball; a sport at which I am horrible. There were tryouts a few weeks before the season started. Practices took place maybe once or twice a week and would trail off as the season progressed. Summertime was always a blast, even if it meant blundering through the baseball season.

Life just did not seem that complicated when I was younger. There was space in the schedule to do nothing and not feel bad about it. There was an actual off-season when it came to sports, except for collecting baseball cards and stale sticks of gum. School work was done at school, mostly. Either way, I do not recall spending much time in front of an open book, unless it was the newest Hardy Boys release from the local library.

However, life today seems very, very different. There seems to be no off-season when it comes to sports anymore. I would venture to say that if you even want to become a starter on the local high school varsity team, then you better have started your career early. Naturally, that career would include summer camps, travel teams, and the never-ending calendar of tournaments and practices.

To succeed in life, students have been convinced that they need to participate in every possible opportunity for well-roundedness. Therefore, clubs and extracurriculars beg for time on the calendar as well. It is not enough to get good grades anymore, especially when your competitor is on two travel sports teams, president of three student organizations, and makes the same grades.

The pressure on students to succeed and "be something amazing" is tremendous. The sad part is most young people will never make a living via sports or organizational involvement. Yet, by the time they graduate and head to the marketplace they will have spent countless hours invested in activities they will most likely never do again. Sadder still, so many of these same people will one day introduce their kids to the same cycle, only it just might be even more intense by that time. Instead of allowing the next generation of children to choose and grow into their own uniqueness, many a parent will live vicariously through their kids.

Some of you may think I am overreacting while others of you may have already noticed the trend and are asking, "When did this happen?" A little bit more each day. Why did this happen? Because we lost the innocence of what childhood is. We let the dream of victory and societal significance overtake our schedule and our children. We pushed kids to grow up faster, be successful sooner, and lose much of the real joy of their childhood. Simply put, we've exchanged God and the gospel for the idols of our choice.

I fight this with our kids. I want them to be successful. I want them to work hard toward a goal. I want them to participate in dance and sports and the like. However, I want them to have the permission to be kids for as long as they can. No one else seems to give them that permission anymore. I do this, if not just for their sake, for the sake of my one-day grandkids. Because I know that if I push my children beyond what is healthy, they will inherit this curse and push their children even more so, unintentionally and unassumingly.

Now follow this line of thought with me as I turn a corner. If one generation after the next pushes children toward sports success and societal significance, then before long childhood will become a myth. I know many might think that to be extreme. However, the National Institute of Mental Health reports that one in four children suffers from an anxiety disorder.[4] The institute also reports that the same twenty-five percent of children will most likely carry that condition with them into adulthood.

Yes, there are chemical issues at work, and diet cannot be let off the hook either. However, I would argue that much of the anxiety we see is heavily environment based. Kids are being forced to grow up quicker than their minds and bodies are truly able to handle.

Children without a childhood would be one sad future reality. As a whole, if life actually got to that point, we might honestly have to say that we had missed the mark; that we were sadly misguided. Families might begin to start a movement in attempts to reclaim the simplicity and innocence of childhood. Organizations against early-aged pressures would begin to pop up. Books would be written about creating space for children to grow up free from over stimulation or over activity. In a sense, if one day we were truly on the edge of childhood extinction, a ground-swell reformation would take place.

A New Reformation Needed?

I wonder if we are on the verge of a similar reformation when it pertains to the church. Church is such a wonderful and worrisome word in today's culture. On one hand, the church is a very visible expression of our great God. On the other hand, today's American church just might be the metaphorical equivalent to a missing childhood. Many people are yet again asking the question: "What is

---

[4] http://www.nimh.nih.gov/health/topics/anxiety-disorders/index.shtml

the church really to be? She has ears, but is she truly hearing what the Heavenly Father is speaking? Is this what Jesus meant for His bride to become? Are we on the verge of yet another reformation?"

I would argue that we are living in a very murky age for the modern church, and mostly because of our own doing. In fact, I would go as far as to say that our lack of listening to the Lord will lead to the demise of today's *modern* church.

Now, before you put this book in the trash and accuse me of not loving the church, let me explain. The reason I even write this at all is because I love the church immensely. I understand this will not be popular, but hear me out. Then I want you to ask yourself the hard questions and see what sticks out, what is stirred up inside of you, and what God might be inviting you to change.

Give Them a King

I had a strange thought the other day about the whole system of church while reading the Old Testament account of Samuel and King Saul found in I Samuel 8. Read the account below. As you do, underline words or phrases that stick out to you. Record your emotional reaction to the text in the margins. Be actively listening to the Lord as you make your way through the passage.

"So Samuel told all the words of the Lord to the people who were asking for a king from him. He said, "These will be the ways of the king who will reign over you: he will take your sons and appoint them to his chariots and to be his horsemen and to run before his chariots. And he will appoint for himself commanders of thousands and commanders of fifties, and some to plow his ground and to reap his harvest, and to make his implements of war and the equipment of his chariots. He will take your daughters to be perfumers and cooks and bakers. He will take the best of your fields and vineyards and olive orchards and give them to his servants. He will take the tenth of your grain and of your vineyards and give it to his officers and to his servants. He will take your male servants and female servants and the best of your young men and your donkeys, and put them to his work. He will take the tenth of your flocks, and you shall be his slaves. And in that day you

will cry out because of your king, whom you have chosen for yourselves, but the Lord will not answer you in that day."

But the people refused to obey the voice of Samuel. And they said, "No! But there shall be a king over us, that we also may be like all the nations, and that our king may judge us and go out before us and fight our battles." And when Samuel had heard all the words of the people, he repeated them in the ears of the LORD. And the LORD said to Samuel, "Obey their voice and make them a king." Samuel then said to the men of Israel, "Go every man to his city." ~ 1 Samuel 8:10-22 ESV

God's chosen people, the Israelites, wanted what every other nation wanted. They wanted a King. Samuel was clear to say that God was their king. However, they would not have it any other way. Sinful pride and stubbornness led to the rejection of their Divine King for a lesser, mortal one. Sadly, the prophet Samuel had to anoint this new human king. Can you imagine having to be obedient to that request? He had to be both angry and heartbroken for the people of Israel.

This was a far cry from what God has intended for His people. He was to be their one true King.

It is such a horrifically sad story to take in. In a way, the Israelites wanted to impeach Yahweh as their leader. The ones purposed for so much more than they lived for and protected like no other people on the planet wanted to change the parameters of their relationship with God in a major way.

What stuns me is their willingness to adopt such a change—even when Samuel prophetically lays out the end results of their decision. None of the conditions Samuel prophesies over the people seems a worthy reason to reject God's reign. Yet, it happened. The nation of Israel was in for a real shock. I would argue that much of Israel's cycle with sin and waywardness in the Old Testament stems from this very moment in their history. They would forever be wrestling with the consequences of their rejection of Yahweh as king. They had ears to hear the divine but chose to listen to the voices of men instead.

Now let's fast forward the story of scripture quite a few years to when a new band of religious zealots rises up in hopes of returning the focus of Israel to its one true king, the Messiah. This group was called the Pharisees. Now, when we think of the Pharisees, we often think about the overly political group of men in the gospel narratives that pushed for the crucifixion of Jesus. While this is a sad truth, that was actually a far cry from the reason this group was formed hundreds of years earlier.

The Pharisees, which means "separate ones," were birthed from a desire to be pure and holy, deeply devoted to God. In third century B.C., the Maccabean revolution took place. Greek influence had overwhelmed the land of Israel. The attempts by the Greek to Hellenize the Jews, forcing them to adopt Greek culture and pagan rituals, bothered the purest of God's people. The result was a group of people dedicated to preserving the Law of Moses; a people choosing to be separate from the carnality of culture.[5]

No one would argue with the intentions of the first Pharisees. However, their methods might not have been the best. In addition to the Law of Moses, the Pharisees created 613 decrees by which God's people were also to live. Most of the decrees were polluted and legalistic interpretations of God's law. They believed the Lord was worthy of their devotion, but their lack of listening for God's voice led to an overly high regard for their traditions. Jesus would eventually chastise this religious practice of God plus tradition in Mark 7:6-8 (ESV).

The Mark 7 text reads: "And he said to them, "Well did Isaiah prophesy of you hypocrites, as it is written: 'This people honors me with their lips, but their heart is far from me; in vain do they worship me, teaching as doctrines the commandments of men. You leave the commandments of God and hold to the tradition of men.'"

In time, the Pharisees had drifted far from the intent of their original charter. Although their attempt was to live "a separate" life and usher in the reign of the Messiah, the Pharisees were soon plagued with a plethora of hypocritical behaviors. In efforts for greater purity, legalism abounded. By the time Jesus and the

---

[5] http://www.bible-history.com/pharisees/

disciples walked the earth, the Pharisees had eroded into a conservative political group completely given over to hypocrisy. They were so conditioned to listening to their own traditions and decrees they could not recognize the person of God before them, let alone hear His voice.

Our Kings and Pharisees

I sometimes wonder if the church has gone the way of king-hungry Israelites and hypocritical Pharisees. Have we become a people that do not listen? Have we developed a slightly deviant system of faith that we are more content with than living in tune with the of voice of the Good Shepherd? Are we living as God intended for us; as individuals and as a church?

There are moments when I think many pastors are like the kings and Pharisees of today, advancing their names and agendas. They operate more like CEOs attempting to grow their church's business instead of pursuing true growth for the kingdom of heaven. I know I was often ensnared by that trap. The flesh likes the ego strokes that being a "successful" pastor can bring.

Churches have become more like the fast-food row of restaurants in a tourist trap town than they are havens of hope and homes of authentic spirituality. You get a combo meal of spiritual nuggets and super-size it with a dose of exciting worship and slick programming. Discipleship is hard to find on the menu. It's a ministry within many churches, not really a lifestyle of the people.

People are too often spoon-fed bites of quasi-truth versus being taught how they might discover truth for themselves. If what sticks out to congregants in the Scriptures is only what their pastor has said, then their emotional response and invitation will be mimics of his as well. Consumeristic tendencies will cause the newest, flashiest church in town to also be the fastest growing. Crowds will gather wherever people's ears are tickled and their faith can be made convenient. Even Paul warned Timothy of this dilemma thousands of years ago.

"For the time is coming when people will not endure sound teaching, but having itching ears they will accumulate for themselves teachers to suit their own passions, and will

turn away from listening to the truth and wander off into myths." ~ 2 Timothy 4:3-4 ESV

You may think I am being harsh, but the statistics for church growth in America might say otherwise. Most Christian denominations have reported a steady decline in membership in the last five years alone. What is worse is that those numbers do not measure kingdom growth either. Just because the number of people in a building seems larger or lesser, does not mean that the hearts of all in attendance are fixed fully on Jesus.

The sad part is I think we have asked for this. We have long prayed and asked God to bless our efforts without asking what He may want of His church. We have been as attractive as we can be when God may simply be asking us to be attentive. In some ways, I question if God has responded affirmatively to these prayers but is it truly what He has wanted? I wonder if Samuel were here today if he would prophesy to us the consequences of our not listening to the voice of the Lord as it pertains to the church, its design, and its purpose.

I wonder if Samuel would say something like:

"You have chosen to listen to the ways of man over the voice of God. Therefore, you will fill buildings but not heaven. You will entertain people but never confront secret sins. You will see behavioral modification but not transformation. People will switch seats, from church to church, but not many will be transferring from the kingdom of darkness to the kingdom of light. You'll train people to sing, 'Lord, Lord' but they won't know Him. You'll have generation after generation without an understanding of scripture's story, resulting in immense biblical illiteracy. You'll work so hard to create a community-friendly image, but more and more people will leave claiming hypocrisy, not authenticity. You'll be religiously busy, but not kingdom minded. You will grow kingdoms, but not the Kingdom. You've chosen the voice of other lovers, even your own, but not His and this is the outcome."

If we neglect the voice of God in our churches, there might come a day when we simply will not recognize it, we will not miss it, and

162

we will not know the difference. Let's pray there never comes a day when churches that hear the voice of God are extinct. May a reformation of listening come first!

- 16 -
A FINAL WORD

And he said, "He who has ears to hear, let him hear."
~ Mark 4:9 ESV

"I like to listen. I have learned a great deal
from listening carefully." ~ Ernest Hemingway

I know the last chapter may have been emotionally heavy to plod through, and rightly so. A warning about what could be is always timely. No one who truly loves the Lord would want to see a rejection of God as King and His voice neglected. However, I want to end with a few words of hope and a series of blessings for the people of God.

Before I close out this meager manifesto about listening, I want to share with you a marvelous nugget of truth I have discovered in my years of practicing the fine art of listening. It is simply this: Listening and responding to the voice of God always fosters a deeper spiritual intimacy with Christ, an intimacy I cannot fully explain with words.

There has been nothing more powerful and humbling than realizing that the God of the universe desires to speak to me. I love it when my son and I get to laugh and talk about life no matter how serious or how goofy. I thoroughly enjoy the conversations my daughter and I have during a shared lunch together. Whenever my wife and I get a night out to eat together, I especially love the time spent talking about what dreams or concerns are on our hearts. Amazingly, as great as all of those moments are, there is nothing that even matches hearing the still small voice of God in my ear. God chose to speak to me, and for that, I am forever grateful.

I do not want to be too narrow focused. God is not chatting with me and me alone. No, He has an equal passion for all His sons and daughters. From heaven, God delivers daily bread to all the saints, past and present, and He never grows weary. Around the throne, the elders hear God's wisdom pour forth. On earth, the Father rebukes the wayward because of His immense love for them. He continually speaks hope, love, and peace into the hearts of those who seek after Him. I guess you could say that God loves being on speaking terms with everyone ever created.

When you consider the population of the planet now and in history past, it is astounding that God can be fully present to all people at all times. No one has to wait in line to have God's full attention. There is never a moment when His love for one saint has to be diminished slightly so that it can grow for another. He loves everyone to the absolute fullest at every moment of every day; He will never love more, never love less. I believe His overwhelming agape love is the reason He desires to reveal Himself is so great.

The very first words of the Bible start with, "In the beginning God created." The first work of God is that of revelation; revealing His power and nature. The final words of the book of Revelation are a prayer asking for God to reveal Himself again. John pens the words that the church cries out today as well: "Come Lord Jesus!" From beginning to end, the Bible speaks of the God who is ever speaking to us.

One day, and I almost tremble with anticipation at the thought of this, we will speak with God face to face. There will be no distance, no hindrances of sin, and God will reveal His glory to us forever. I don't know about you, but my heart cries out with the revelatory prayer of John, "Come Lord Jesus!"

Blessed Be...

Quite a few years back, I became familiar with a pastor who ended his sermons with a Hebrew-style blessing. I recall being struck with the powerful hope that was generated in me whenever I would hear those blessings. It was as if he was proclaiming hope over his congregation. The people sat in their pews receiving divine inspiration to live life, greater attuned to the work of God. To be honest, that positive method of closing a challenging sermon has changed the way that I like to close out my messages as well. Therefore, I will conclude the book, this message, with this prayer of blessing.

May We Be

May we be congregations of groups small enough to care. May we practice learning to listen to God's great voice in groups together. May that listening assist us in learning to love each other as God has loved us.

May we be churches big enough to dare. May we all be pastors and priests boldly reaching out to our marketplaces, workplaces, community groups, and everyday relationships with the truths that have stuck out to us, moved us, and called us to obedience.

May we be a people that are real enough to reveal. May what God is doing in our hearts be so real and powerful that we are willing to share it with the lost and the found— no matter how vulnerable it makes us or how raw it feels.

May we listen enough to hear. May our ability to listen to both Holy Spirit and our fellow brothers and sisters in Christ become so honed that we become wise guides for others in their journey of faith. May we aid the conflicted and help the doubter find faith.

May we die in order to be raised. May our lives truly be marked by the obedience found in the dying surrender of self so that we might be raised to life eternal.

May we disciple enough to see true spiritual descendants. May we see generations after generations of active listeners, children of God who both hear and love the wooing of the Good Shepherd.

Finally, *may we have ears to hear*. May we never stop listening for the wonderful voice of our great God.

APPENDIX

This portion of the book contains sample *Sticks, Stars, and Signs* journaling experiences as well as a copy of the liturgy guide used by *Lectio Divina* groups. It is my sincere hope that these tools will serve as an aid in your exploration of the God of the Scriptures, personally and communally.

For more information about how to implement these tools into individual life and ministry practice, please contact the Shawn Stutz Training Group. Shawn is also available to lead interactive *"I Have Ears"* seminars and weekends for church staffs, ministry leadership groups, and even whole congregations.

Contact Information:
Shawn Stutz Training Group   ShawnStutz.com
PO Box 1221   865.313.5520
Seymour, Tennessee 37865

* * * * * * * * * * * *

STICKS, STARS, and SIGNS SAMPLES

When practicing Sticks, Stars, and Signs in a Lectio Group, it is best to record each of the separate steps in a journal rather than performing them mentally only. Journaling the findings achieved during listening allows for personal reflection to take place later. A written synopsis will also help each participant be able to articulate more clearly God's messages to them when the time comes to share with others. Remember, the listening and reflecting are important. Yet, the more one verbalizes exactly what God has spoken to him or her, the more a culture of God-listening and expectancy will be created.

Before we begin, it is important to understand the Key for these samples. A dash (—) will be used to indicate the Stick aspect of listening to the Scriptures. An asterisk (*) will be used to highlight the emotional piece of each *Lectio Divina* time. Finally, the greater than symbol (>) will designate the invitation one hears from the Lord.

The samples given in the following pages are taken from my journals; recorded to help me hear and respond to the voice of God in my life. Read, partake as well, and enjoy!

USING THE LECTIO LITURGY GUIDE

All points of the liturgy guide below are spoken aloud and in unison with everyone in the *Lectio Divina* gathering. Obviously, the only points of the liturgy not spoken aloud are the places labeled "silent prayer."

Following each of the three scripture readings, a moment of silence will be observed for participants to reflect on what was read, what God is speaking, and give proper time for journaling of each *Lectio Divina* segment.

The scripture reading for the day can be found in any lectionary. Lectionaries are pre-chosen lists of Scriptures from various portions of the Bible which are to be read daily. They can be found online for free. One such easy to use lectionary can be found here:

http://www.esvbible.org/devotions/bcp/

Feel Free to Make Copies of the Lectio Divina Liturgy Guide for either Personal or Lectio Group Gatherings.

LECTIO DIVINA LITURGY GUIDE[*]

Opening Prayer
In the name of the Father and the Son and the Holy Spirit, Amen.

Seeking God (Psalm 27:4)
One thing I have asked of the Lord, this is what I seek:
That I may dwell in the house of the Lord all the days of my life,
to behold the beauty of the Lord and to seek Him in His temple.

Silent Prayer of Seeking

Declaration of Faith
To whom shall we go? You have the words of eternal life,
And we have believed and have come to know that
You are the Holy One of God.
Praise to You, Lord Jesus Christ, King of endless glory.

Scripture Reading & Meditation (Found in Daily Lectionary)

Canticle (Adaptation of St. Patrick's Breastplate)
Christ, as a light illumine and guide me.
Christ, as shield overshadow me.
Christ under me; Christ over me;
Christ beside me; on my left and my right.
This day be within and without me,
lowly and meek, yet all powerful.
Be in the heart of each to whom I speak;
In the mouth of each who speaks unto me.
This day be within and without me,
lowly and meek, yet all powerful.
Christ, as a light; Christ as a shield;
Christ beside me on my left and my right.
            Silent Prayer for those on your left and your right

Closing Prayer
In the name of the Father and the Son and the Holy Spirit, Amen.

---

[*]*Adapted from Celtic Daily Prayer: Prayers and Readings from the Northumbria Community, page 17-19*

SAMPLE ONE

Reading One: **STICKS**

— *"loses his life for me"*

Reading Two: **STARS**

* I felt *included*, even *invited*. I identified with the disciples most in this passage. Jesus huddled up with His disciples and shared a message very important and crucial to His mission on earth. In many ways, I felt included in that time. I felt invited into a conversation of challenge and truth; like it was an extension of Jesus' time with the disciples.

* I also felt *hesitant* or *unwilling*. The cost of following Jesus is high; it demands all of me. I felt hesitant or unwilling because there are times when my attempts to follow Christ's commands seem minimal or non-existent in my life.

Reading Three: **SIGNS**

> "Shawn, I AM LIFE. Your life apart from me is an inheritance of death. Lose your version of life that you may gain mine. Denial isn't negative, it's needed. The inheritance is life."

* * * * * * * * * * * * *

*Try practicing the **Sticks, Stars, and Signs** method with this passage using your own journal or use the **I Have Ears: Listening for God** guideline provided.*

```
┌─────────────────────────────────────────────────────────┐
│                                                           │
│  PASSAGE:                          DATE:                  │
│                                                           │
└─────────────────────────────────────────────────────────┘
```

LISTENING FOR GOD

Reading One: **STICKS** *(Word or Phrase)*

—

—

Reading Two: **STARS** *(What stirs you emotionally?)*

*

*

*

Reading Three: **SIGNS** *(What is the invitation Jesus has for you?)*

>

>

| PASSAGE: Psalm 23 | DATE: March 4 |

SAMPLE TWO

Reading One: **STICKS**

— *"He leads me (in paths of righteousness for His name's sake)"*

Reading Two: **STARS**

* I felt *nervous*, or more accurately, *untrusting*. God has the right to lead me on a pathway I don't desire. This is where the nervousness arises. Or as stated previously, the better word to describe these feelings would be untrusting. The question is nagging me: do I truly trust God to lead me in any pathway He wants for me?

* I felt *compelled*. The reason this word came to mind is pretty straightforward: If righteousness and glory to God are the results of me surrendering my life to follow His pathway, then I simply feel compelled toward obedience. The beautiful part was the feeling didn't in any way feel negative, but instead powerfully positive.

Reading Three: **SIGNS**

> "Shawn, trust Me. I have and always have had the wisest way for you to live. The pathway, with mountains and valleys, will bring Me glory and bring you life abundant. Trust Me."

* * * * * * * * * * * * *

*Try practicing the **Sticks, Stars, and Signs** method with this passage using your own journal or use the **I Have Ears: Listening for God** guideline provided.*

```
┌─────────────────────────────────────────────────────────┐
│  PASSAGE:                           DATE:                 │
└─────────────────────────────────────────────────────────┘
```

LISTENING FOR GOD

Reading One: **STICKS** *(Word or Phrase)*

—

—

Reading Two: **STARS** *(What stirs you emotionally?)*

*

*

*

Reading Three: **SIGNS** *(What is the invitation Jesus has for you?)*

>

>

SAMPLE THREE

Reading One: **STICKS**

— *"I don't know the man"*

Reading Two: **STARS**

* I felt *sadness*. I felt a heavy sadness at seeing the courage of Peter drained during his adamant denial of Jesus as both his friend and Lord. That same sadness was eventually Peter's sadness as he left the courtyard weeping bitterly.

Reading Three: **SIGNS**

> "Shawn, draw so close to Me that any betrayal of Me would feel like self-betrayal. Help those who would say, 'I don't know the man' catch a greater glimpse of Me."

* * * * * * * * * * * * *

*Try practicing the **Sticks, Stars, and Signs** method with this passage using your own journal or use the **I Have Ears: Listening for God** guideline provided.*

PASSAGE:	DATE:

LISTENING FOR GOD

Reading One: **STICKS** *(Word or Phrase)*

—

—

Reading Two: **STARS** *(What stirs you emotionally?)*

*

*

*

Reading Three: **SIGNS** *(What is the invitation Jesus has for you?)*

>

>

PASSAGE: Matthew 28:16-20	DATE: April 14

SAMPLE FOUR

Reading One: **STICKS**

— *"the mountain to which Jesus had directed"*

Reading Two: **STARS**

* I felt *glad* listening to this text. There was a direction given, a location even. My life is in need of direction in a big way right now.

* I also felt *comfort*. All of the activities listed in this passage — (disciples) "went," "saw," "worshipped," "doubted," (go) "make disciples," "baptizing," "teaching" — all happen in the present or future presence of Christ "with" them.

Reading Three: **SIGNS**

> "Shawn, 1) go to the place I have directed for you, 2) when you see Me there, worship and don't doubt, 3) wait for the next *make disciples* opportunity, 4) know that I am with you."

* * * * * * * * * * * * *

*Try practicing the **Sticks, Stars, and Signs** method with this passage using your own journal or use the **I Have Ears** guideline provided.*